AA Essential

Russian
phrase book

AA Publishing

Contents

English edition prepared by First Edition Translations Ltd, Great Britain

Designed and produced by AA Publishing

Distributed in the United Kingdom by AA Publishing, Norfolk House, Priestley Road, Basingstoke, Hampshire RG24 9NY

First published in 1995 as Wat & Hoe Russisch,
© Uitgeverij Kosmos bv - Utrecht/Antwerpen

Van Dale Lexicografie bv - Utrecht/Antwerpen

This edition © The Automobile Association 1997

A CIP catalogue record for this book is available from the British Library

ISBN: 0 7495 1476 0

Published by AA Publishing (a trading name of Automobile Association Developments Limited, whose registered office is Norfolk House, Priestley Road, Basingstoke, Hampshire RG24 9NY. Registered number 1878835).

Typeset by Anton Graphics Ltd, Andover, Hampshire.

Printed and bound by G. Canale C.SpA, Torino, Italy.

Photocredits for front cover: Dolls, Moscow, AA Photo Library (J. Arnold); street musician, Moscow, AA Photo Library (J. Arnold); Church of Resurrection, St Petersburg, AA Photo Library (K. Paterson)

Introduction

● **Welcome to the AA's new Essential Phrase Books series, covering the most popular European languages and containing everything you'd expect from a comprehensive language series. They're concise, accessible and easy to understand, and you'll find them indispensable on your trip abroad.**

Each guide is divided into 15 themed sections and starts with a pronunciation table which explains the phonetic pronunciation to all the words and phrases you'll need to know for your trip, while at the back of the book is an extensive word list and grammar guide which will help you construct basic sentences in your chosen language.

Throughout the book you'll come across coloured boxes with a 🗪 beside them. These are designed to help you if you can't understand what your listener is saying to you. Hand the book over to them and encourage them to point to the appropriate answer to the question you are asking.

Other coloured boxes in the book - this time without the symbol - give alphabetical listings of themed words with their English translations beside them.

For extra clarity, we have put all English words and phrases in black, foreign language terms in red and their phonetic pronunciation in italic.

This phrase book covers all subjects you are likely to come across during the course of your visit, from reserving a room for the night to ordering food and drink at a restaurant and what to do if your car breaks down or you lose your traveller's cheques and money. With over 2,000 commonly used words and essential phrases at your fingertips you can rest assured that you will be able to get by in all situations, so let the Essential Phrase Book become your passport to a secure and enjoyable trip!

Pronunciation table

The most important thing about the pronunciation of Russian words is their stress. Each Russian word longer than one syllable has one main stress, so getting the stress right maximises the chances of the person you are talking to recognising the word you are saying. In this phrasebook the stressed syllable is indicated in bold type in the English transcription. Occasionally you will see a word of only one syllable stressed: this conveys meaning to the whole sentence, for instance turning it from a statement into a question.

The Russian words in this phrasebook have been transcribed in a way that is as close to the look of English words as possible. In order to imitate some special Russian sounds, in our transcription we have used the following conventions:

kh	is pronounced as **ch** in Scottish **loch**
air	is pronounced as in **fair**
igh	is pronounced as in **high**
or	when followed by a hyphen has a silent **r**
zh	is pronounced like the **s** in **treasure**
y	when not followed by a vowel stands for the unique Russian vowel **ы** (see Russian alphabet below)

The Russian alphabet

А	а	long, as in **father**
Б	б	**b** as in **book**
В	в	**v** as in **vote**
Г	г	**g** as in **good**
Д	д	**d** as in **day**
Е	е	**yeh** as in **yell**
Ё	ё	**yoh** as in **yonder**
Ж	ж	**s** as in **treasure**
З	з	**z** as in **zone**
И	и	**ee** as in **meet**
Й	й	**y** as in **boy**
К	к	**k** as in **kind**
Л	л	**l** as in **look**
М	м	**m** as in **man**
Н	н	**n** as in **note**
О	о	long, as in **port**
П	п	**p** as in **pen**
Р	р	**r** rolled as in **Rory**
С	с	**s** as in **speak**
Т	т	**t** as in **too**
У	у	**oo** as in **oodles**
Ф	ф	**f** as in **fire**
Х	х	**ch** as in Scottish **loch**
Ц	ц	**ts** as in **carts**
Ч	ч	**ch** as in **cheep**
Ш	ш	**sh** as in **short**
Щ	щ	**shch** as in **pushchair**
	ъ	**hard** sign, not pronounced
	ы	very hard **i** as in **igloo**
	ь	**soft** sign, not pronounced
Э	э	**e** as in **men**
Ю	ю	**yu** as in **Yukon**
Я	я	**ya** as in **yard**

Useful lists

1 .1 **T**oday or tomorrow?

What day is it today? _____	Какой сегодня день?
	Kakoy sivordnya dyen?
Today's Monday_____	Сегодня понедельник
	Sivordnya punidyelneek
– Tuesday_____	вторник
	ftorneek
– Wednesday _____	среда
	sridar
– Thursday_____	четверг
	chitvyairk
– Friday_____	пятница
	pyatnitsa
– Saturday _____	суббота
	sooborta
– Sunday _____	воскресенье
	vuskrisyaynya
in January _____	в январе
	vyanvaryeh
since February _____	с февраля
	sfevralya
in spring_____	весной
	visnoy
in summer_____	летом
	lyetum
in autumn _____	осенью
	orsinyu
in winter_____	зимой
	zeemoy
1997_____	тысяча девятьсот девяносто седьмой год
	tysicha divutsort divyanorsta sidmoy gort
the twentieth century _____	двадцатый век
	dvutsarty vyek
What's the date today? ___	Какое сегодня число?
	Kakoya sivordnya cheesslor?
Today's the 23rd _____	Сегодня двадцать третье
	Sivordnya dvartsut tryaytyeh
Monday 2 November _____	понедельник, второе ноября тысяча
1998	девятьсот девяносто восьмого года
	punidyelneek, fturroyeh nuyubbrya tysicha
	divutsort divyanorsta vussmorva gorda
in the morning _____	утром
	ootrum
in the afternoon _____	днём
	dnyom
in the evening _____	вечером
	vaychirum
at night_____	ночью
	norchyu
this morning _____	сегодня утром
	sivordnya ootrum
this afternoon _____	сегодня днём
	sivordnya dnyom

this evening	сегодня вечером
	sivordnya vaychirum
tonight	сегодня ночью
	sivordnya norchyu
last night	прошлой ночью
	prorshloy norchyu
this week	на этой неделе
	na etoy nidyaylye
next month	в следующем месяце
	fslyedooyushchem myaysyetseh
last year	в прошлом году
	vprorshlum guddoo
next...	следующий...
	slyedooyushchee...
in...days/weeks/	через...дней/недель/месяцев/лет
months/years	*chayruss...dnyay/nidyell/myaysyetsev/lyet*
...weeks ago	...недель тому назад
	...nidyell tummoo nazat
day off	выходной день
	vykhudnoy dyen

1.2 Bank holidays

● **The most important** national ('Bank') holidays in Russia are:

1 January	New Year (Новый Год, *Norvy Gort*)
8 March	International Women's Day (Международный женский день, *Myezhdoonarordny zhenski dyen*)
1 May	May Day (Праздник Первого Мая, *Prarznik pyairvuvva mighya*)
9 May	Victory Day (День Победы, *Dyen Pubbyedy*)
12 June	Independence Day (День независимости России, *Dyen nyezaveessimusti Russee-ee*)

On these days, banks and government institutions are closed.
Religious festivals are also being increasingly observed.
The Russian Orthodox Church still follows the Julian Calendar, which is thirteen days behind the Western Gregorian calendar. The most important Russian Orthodox festivals are:

Christmas	7 January (Рождество, *Ruzhdistvor*)
Easter	May coincide with Western Easter, (Пасха, *Parskha*), be one week later, or five weeks later
Ascension Day	Forty days after Easter (Вознесение, *Vuznisyayniya*)
Whitsun	Fifty days after Easter (Троицын день, *Troyitsin dyen*)

1.3 What time is it?

What time is it?	Который час?
	Kutory chass?
It's nine o'clock	Девять часов
	Dyevit chassorf
– five past ten	Десять часов пять минут
	Dyesit chassorf pyat minoot
– a quarter past eleven	Одиннадцать часов пятнадцать минут
	Udeenatsat chassorf pitnatsat minoot
– twenty past twelve	Двенадцать часов двадцать минут
	Dvinartsat chassorf dvartsat minoot

– half past one _____	Половина второго	*Puluvveena fturorva*
– twenty–five to three_____	Без двадцати пяти три	*Byes dvutsutee pitee tree*
– a quarter to four _____	Без четверти четыре	*Byes chaytvertee chiteery*
– ten to five _____	Без десяти пять	*Byes disyatee pyat*
– twelve noon_____	Двенадцать часов дня	*Dvinartsut chassorf dnya*
– midnight _____	Двенадцать часов ночи	*Dvinartsut chassorf norchi*
half an hour _____	полчаса	*polchassah*
What time? _____	В котором часу?	*Fkutorum chassoo?*
What time can I come _____ round?	В котором часу мне прийти?	*Fkutorum chassoo mnyeh preetee?*
At... _____	В...	*V...*
After... _____	После...	*Porslyeh...*
Before... _____	До...	*Dor...*
Between...and... _____	Между...и...	*Myezhdoo...ee...*
From...to... _____	С...до...	*S...dor...*
In...minutes _____	Через...минут	*Chayruss...minoot*
– ...hours _____	Через...часов	*Chayruss...chassorf*
– a quarter of an hour ____	Через четверть часа	*Chayruss chaytvert chassah*
– three quarters of_____ an hour	Через сорок пять минут	*Chayruss soruk pyat minoot*
early/late _____	Слишком рано/поздно	*Sleeshkum rarno/porzna*
on time_____	вовремя	*vorvremya*
summertime _____	летнее время	*lyetnyeya vraymya*
wintertime _____	зимнее время	*zeemnyeya vraymya*

1.4 One, two, three...

0 _____	ноль/нуль	*norl/nool*
1 _____	один	*udeen*
2 _____	два	*dvah*
3 _____	три	*tree*
4 _____	четыре	*chiteery*
5 _____	пять	*pyat*
6 _____	шесть	*shest*
7 _____	семь	*syem*
8 _____	восемь	*vorsim*
9 _____	девять	*dyevit*

10	десять	*dyesit*
11	одиннадцать	*udeenatsut*
12	двенадцать	*dvinartsut*
13	тринадцать	*trinartsut*
14	четырнадцать	*chiteernatsut*
15	пятнадцать	*pitnartsut*
16	шестнадцать	*shistnartsut*
17	семнадцать	*simnartsut*
18	восемнадцать	*vusimnartsut*
19	девятнадцать	*divitnartsut*
20	двадцать	*dvartsut*
21	двадцать один	*dvartsut udeen*
22	двадцать два	*dvartsut dvah*
30	тридцать	*treetsut*
31	тридцать один	*treetsut udeen*
32	тридцать два	*treetsut dvah*
40	сорок	*soruk*
50	пятьдесят	*pitdisyaht*
60	шестьдесят	*shistdisyaht*
70	семьдесят	*syemdisyut*
80	восемьдесят	*vorsimdisyut*
90	девяносто	*divyanorsto*
100	сто	*stor*
101	сто один	*stor udeen*
110	сто десять	*stor dyesit*
120	сто двадцать	*stor dvartsut*
200	двести	*dvyaysti*
300	триста	*treesta*
400	четыреста	*chiteerista*
500	пятьсот	*pitsort*
600	шестьсот	*shistsort*
700	семьсот	*simsort*
800	восемьсот	*vusimsort*
900	девятьсот	*divutsort*
1000	тысяча	*tysicha*
1100	тысяча сто	*tysicha stor*
2000	две тысячи	*dvyeh tysichi*
10,000	десять тысяч	*dyesit tysich*
100,000	сто тысяч	*stor tysich*
1,000,000	миллион	*meeliorn*
1st	первый	*pyairvy*
2nd	второй	*fturoy*
3rd	третий	*traytyee*
4th	чевёртый	*chitvyorty*
5th	пятый	*pyarty*
6th	шестой	*shistoy*
7th	седьмой	*sidmoy*
8th	восьмой	*vusmoy*
9th	девятый	*divyahty*
10th	десятый	*disyahty*
11th	одиннадцатый	*udeenatsuty*
12th	двенадцатый	*dvinartsuty*
13th	тринадцатый	*trinartsuty*
14th	четырнадцатый	*chityrnatsuty*
15th	пятнадцатый	*pitnartsuty*
16th	шестнадцатый	*shistnartsuty*

17th _____	семнадцатый	*simnartsuty*
18th _____	восемнадцатый	*vusimnartsuty*
19th _____	девятнадцатый	*divitnartsuty*
20th _____	двадцатый	*dvutsarty*
21st _____	двадцать первый	*dvartsut pyairvy*
22nd _____	двадцать второй	*dvartsut fturoy*
30th _____	тридцатый	*tritsarty*
100th _____	сотый	*sorty*
1000th _____	тысячный	*tysichny*

once _____	раз	*rass*
twice _____	дважды	*dvarzhdy*
double _____	вдвойне	*vdvoynyeh*
triple _____	втройне	*vtroynyeh*
half _____	половина	*puluvveena*
a quarter _____	четверть	*chaytvert*
a third _____	треть	*trayt*
a couple, a few, some _____	несколько	*nyeskulka*

2+4=6 _____	два плюс четыре равняется шести
	dvah plyus chiteery ravnyaitsa shistee
4-2=2 _____	четыре минус два равняется двум
	chiteery meenus dvah ravnyaitsa dvoom
2x4=8 _____	два на четыре равняется восьми
	dvah na chiteery ravnyaitsa vusmee
4÷2=2 _____	четыре разделить на два равняется двум
	chiteery razdeleet na dvah ravnyaitsa dvoom
odd/even _____	чётно/нечётно
	chotna/nichotna
total _____	в итоге
	veetorgyeh
6x9 _____	шесть на девять
	shest na dyevit

🔊 .5 The weather

Is the weather going to be good/bad?	Будет хорошая/плохая погода?
	Boodyetkhurorshaya/plukhaya pugorda?
Is it going to get colder/hotter?	Похолодает?/Потеплеет?
	Pukhulludighet?/Puttiplayet?
What temperature is it going to be?	Сколько будет градусов?
	Skorlka boodyet grahdoosoff?
Is it going to rain?	Будет дождь?
	Boodyet dorzht?
Is there going to be a storm?	Будет буря?
	Boodyet boorya?
Is it going to snow?	ПойдСт снег?
	Puydyot snyek?
Is it going to freeze?	Будет мороз?
	Boodyet murorss?
Is the thaw setting in?	Будет оттепель?
	Boodyet ort-tipyel?
Is it going to be foggy?	Будет туман?
	Boodyet toomarn?

Is there going to be a _____ thunderstorm?	Будет гроза? *Boodyet gruzzah?*
The weather's changing ___	Погода меняется *Pugorda minyayetsa*
It's cooling down _____	Холодает *Khullud-eye-yet*
What's the weather _____ going to be like today/ tomorrow?	Какая будет сегодня/завтра погода? *Kakaya boodyet sivordnya/zarftra pugorda?*

погода weather	солнечно sunny	временами occasionally
мороз frost	град hail	максимальная/миним альнаятемпература
безоблачно clear	сыро wet	около maximum/minimum
облачно cloudy	дождь rain	temperature
ветер wind	тепло warm	about
прохладно cool	душно close	временами дождь/снег
ветрено windy	туман fog	occasionally rain/snow
свежо fresh	(очень) жарко (very) hot	облачная погода с прояснениями
сильный ветер strong wind	(очень) холодно (very) cold	cloudy with clear intervals
снег snow	...градусов ниже/выше нуля	северный/восточный /южный/
гололедица black ice	...degrees below/above zero	западный ветер winds northerly/easterly/ southerly/westerly

.6 Here, there...

See also 5.1 Asking for directions

here/there _____	здесь/там *zdyess/tarm*
somewhere/nowhere _____	где-то/нигде *'gdyeh-ta/neegdyeh*
everywhere _____	везде *vyizdyeh*
far away/nearby _____	далеко/близко *dalikor/bleeska*
right/left _____	направо/налево *nuprarva/nulyeva*
to the right/left of _____	справа/слева от *sprarva/slyeva ut*
straight ahead _____	прямо *pryarma*
via _____	через *chayruss*
in _____	в *v*

English	Russian	Transliteration
on	на	*nah*
under	под	*pudd*
against	против	*prorteef*
opposite	напротив	*nahprorteef*
next to	возле	*vorzlyeh*
near	у	*oo*
in front of	перед	*pyayrut*
in the centre	в середине	*fsirideenyeh*
forward	вперёд	*fpiryot*
at the bottom	внизу	*vneezoo*
down/downwards	вниз	*vneess*
at the top	наверху	*navirkhoo*
up/upwards	наверх	*nuvyairkh*
inside	внутри	*vnootree*
into the inside	внутрь	*vnootr*
on the outside	снаружи	*snaroozhy*
from behind	сзади	*s-zardee*
back/ago	назад	*nuzzaht*
at the front	впереди	*vpiridee*
at the back	позади	*puzzudee*
in the north	на севере	*nah sayveeryeh*
to the south	на юг	*nah yook*
from the west	с запада	*s-zarpudda*
from the east	с востока	*s-vustorka*
to the...of	на...от	*nah...ort...*

.7 What does that sign say?

See 5.4 Traffic signs

Useful lists

администрация
manager

купаться
 воспрещается
swimming
 prohibited

вода не для
питья
no drinking water

лестница
stairs

вход
entrance

лифт
lift

вход бесплатный/
свободный
free admission

место для
 инвалидов и
 пассажиров с
 детьми
These seats are
 reserved for disabled
 persons or
 passengers with
 children

высокое напряжение
high voltage

выход
exit

мужской туалет
gents/gentlemen

женский туалет
ladies

не беспокоить
do not disturb

заказано
reserved

не влезай, убьёт
keep out: danger to life

закрыт на обед
closed for lunch

не высовываться
do not lean out

закрыт на
 (капитальный)
 ремонт
closed for (major)
 repairs

не курить
no smoking

запасный выход
emergency exit

не работает
out of order

запасный тормоз
emergency brake

не трогать
please do
 not touch

запрещено
 разжигать костёр
no open fires

огнеопасно
fire hazard

запрещено для
 домашних
 животных
no pets allowed

опасно
danger

осторожно
caution

информация
information

осторожно, злая
 собака
beware of the dog

к поездам
to the trains

осторожно,
 окрашено
wet paint

к себе/от себя
pull/push

открыто/закрыто
open/closed

касса
pay here

питьевая вода
drinking water

платформа
platform

свободных мест
нет
full/sold out/no
 vacancies

по газону не
 ходить
keep off the
 grass

сдаётся в
 наём
for hire

пожарная
 лестница
fire escape

смертельно
 опасно
danger to life

посторонним вход
 воспрещён
no entry

фотографировать
 воспрещается
no photographs

продаётся
for sale

частная
 собственность
private property

путь
track (platform)

частное владение
no trespassing

рабочее время
opening hours

регистратура
escalator

эскалатор
reception

этаж
floor

.8 Telephone alphabet

а	(ah)	как Анна	kukk **Ar**na
б	(beh)	как Борис	kukk Bur**ree**ss
в	(veh)	как Виктор	kukk **Vee**ktur
г	(geh)	как Григорий	kukk Gree**go**ree
д	(deh)	как Дмитрий	kukk Dm**ee**tree
е	(yeh)	как Елена	kukk Yel**yay**na
ё	(yoh)	как Ёлка	kukk **Yo**lka
ж	(zheh)	как Женя	kukk **Zhe**nya
з	(zeh)	как Зоя	kukk **Zoy**-ya
и	(ee)	как Ирина	kukk Ir**ee**na
й	(ee kr**art**koye)	как Йод	kukk Yot
к	(kah)	как Константин	kukk Kunstan**teen**
л	(ell)	как Лиза	kukk **Lee**za
м	(em)	как Мария	kukk Mur**ree**ya
н	(en)	как Наташа	kukk Nu**tar**sha
о	(or)	как Ольга	kukk **Or**lga
п	(peh)	как Пётр	kukk Pyotr
р	(air)	как Руслан	kukk Rooss**lar**n
с	(ess)	как Семён	kukk Sim**yon**
т	(teh)	как Татьяна	kukk Tutee**yar**na
у	(oo)	как Украина	kukk Ookra**ee**na
ф	(eff)	как Фёдор	kukk F**yo**dur
х	(khah)	как Харьков	kukk Khar**kuff**
ц	(tseh)	как Царица	kukk Tsar**ee**tsa
ч	(cheh)	как Чехов	kukk **Che**khuff
ш	(shah)	как Шура	kukk **Shoo**ra
щ	(shchah)	как Щука	kukk Shch**oo**ka
ъ	(tv**yor**dy znark)	} not used at beginning of word	
ы	(y)		
ь	(m**yar**khki znark)		
э	(eh)	как Эрик	kukk **Ai**reek
ю	(yoo)	как Юрий	kukk **Yoo**ree
я	(yah)	как Яна	kukk **Yah**na

.9 Personal details

Russians have a single forename and a surname, and in between a name that is derived from their father's forename (the so-called patronymic). For example:

Пётр Иванович Кузнецов
*Pyotr Iva**r**novich Kooznits**or**ff*
Анна Петровна Кузнецова
*Ar**na** Pitr**or**vna Kooznits**or**va*

The patronymic is most often used preceded by the forename as a polite form of address.

surname _____	фамилия
	*fam**ee**liya*
forename _____	имя
	***ee**mya*
patronymic _____	отчество
	***ort**chistva*
initials _____	инициалы
	*initsee**ar**ly*

address (street/number) ___	адрес (улица/дом)
	ardriss (ooleetsa/dorm)
post code/town _____	индекс/местожительство
	eendiks/myestozheetelstva
sex (male/female) _____	пол (м/ж)
	porl (m/zh)
nationality _____	национальность
	nutsiunarlnust
date of birth _____	дата рождения
	darta ruzhdyayniya
place of birth _____	место рождения
	myesta ruzhdyayniya
occupation_____	профессия
	pruffaysiya
married/single/divorced____	женат (замужем) / не женат (не замужем)/
(bracketed form when	разведен (разведена)
woman speaking)	*zhinart(zarmoozhum) /nyeh zhinart (nyeh*
	zarmoooozhum) /ruzvidyon (ruzvidyinar)
widowed m/f_____	вдовец/вдова
	vduvyets/vduvvar
(number of) children _____	дети
	dyayti
passport/identity _____	номер паспорта / номер водительских
card/driving licence	прав
number	*normir parssporta / normir vudeety-*
	ilskeekh prahff
place and date of issue ___	место и дата выдачи
	myesta ee darta vyduchi

Courtesies

Courtesies

2 .1 **G**reetings

Hello, Mr Smith _____ Здравствуйте, господин Смит
Zdrarstvootyeh, guspuddeen Smeet

Hello, Mrs Jones _____ Здравствуйте, госпожа Джонс
Zdrarstvootyeh, guspuzhar Dzhorns

Hello, Peter _____ Привет, Питер
Preevyet, Peetir

Hi, Helen _____ Привет, Хелен
Preevyet, Khelin

Good morning, madam ____ Доброе утро, госпожа
Dorbroya ootra, guspuzhar

Good afternoon, sir _____ Добрый день, господин
Dorbry dyen, guspuddeen

Good evening_____ Добрый вечер
Dorbry vaychir

How are you? _____ Как поживаете? Как дела?
  How's things? *Kukk puzhivahyetyeh? Kukk dillar?*

Fine, thank you, _____ Хорошо, а вы?
  and you? *Khurushor, ah vy?*

Very well _____ Отлично
Utleechna

Not very well _____ Не очень
Nyeh orchin

Not too bad_____ Ничего
Nichivor

I'd better be going_____ Я, пожалуй, пойду
Ya, puzharlooy, puydoo

I have to be going _____ Я должен идти. Меня ждут.
  Someone's waiting *Ya dorlzhun eed-tee. Minya zhdoot*
  for me

Bye!_____ Пока!
Pukkah!

Goodbye _____ До свидания
Duh svidarniya

See you soon _____ До скорого
Duh skorova

See you in a little while/ ___ Пока
  cheerio *Pukkah*

Sleep well _____ Спокойной ночи
Spukkoyny norchee

Good night _____ Доброй ночи
Dorbry norchee

All the best _____ Всего наилучшего
Vsivor na-eeloochshiva

Have fun_____ Всего хорошего
Vsivor khororshiva

Good luck _____ Удачи
Oodarchee

Have a nice holiday _____ Хорошего отдыха
Khurorshiva ortdykha

Have a good trip _____ Счастливого пути
Schastleevuvva pootee

Thank you, you too _____	Спасибо, вам того же
	Spaseeba, varm tuvvor zheh
Say hello to...for me _____	Привет...
	Preevyet...

2.2 How to ask a question

Who? _____	Кто?
	Ktor?
Who's that? _____	Кто это?
	Ktor eta?
What? _____	Что?
	Shtor?
What's there to _____ see here?	Что здесь можно посмотреть?
	Shtor zdyess morzhna pusmutrayt?
What kind of hotel _____ is that?	Что это за гостиница?
	Shtor eta zah gusteenitsa?
Where? _____	Где?
	Gdyeh?
Where's the toilet? _____	Где туалет?
	Gdyeh too-alyet?
Where are you going? _____	Куда вы идёте?
	Koodar by eedyotye?
Where are you from? _____	Откуда вы?
	Utkoodah vy?
How? _____	Как?
	Kark?
How far is that? _____	Как это далеко?
	Kukk eta dalikor?
How long does that take? __	Сколько это длится?
	Skorlka eta dleetsa?
How long is the trip? _____	Сколько длится путешествие?
	Skorlka dleetsa pootyeshestviya?
How much? _____	Сколько?
	Skorlka?
How much is this? _____	Сколько это стоит?
	Skorlka eta stor-eet?
What time is it? _____	Который час?
	Kutory chass?
Which one? _____	Который? Которые?
Which ones?	*Kutory? Kutory-yeh?*
Which glass is mine? _____	Которая рюмка для меня?
	Kutoraya ryoomka dlya minya?
When? _____	Когда?
	Kugdar?
When are you leaving? _____	Когда вы уезжаете?
	Kugdar vy oo-yizhah-yityeh?
Why? _____	Почему?
	Puchimoo?
Could you...me? _____	Не могли бы вы...?
	Nyeh muglee by vy...?
Could you help me, _____ please?	Не могли бы вы мне помочь?
	Nyeh muglee by vy mnyeh pummorch?
Could you point that _____ out to me?	Не могли бы вы мне показать?
	Nyeh muglee by vy mnyeh pukkuzzart?

Could you come _____ with me, please?	Не могли бы вы пойти со мной? *Nyeh muglee by vy puytee sumnoy?*
Could you..._____	Вы можете...? *Vy morzhityeh...?*
Could you reserve some ___ tickets for me, please?	Вы можете заказать для меня билеты? *Vy morzhityeh zukkuzzart dlya minya bilyety?*
Do you know...? _____	Вы знаете...? *Vy znahyityeh...?*
Do you know another_____ hotel, please?	Вы не знаете другую гостиницу? *Vy nyeh znahyityeh droogooyu gusteenit-soo?*
Do you have a...?_____	У вас есть...? *Oo vass yest...?*
Do you have a _____ vegetarian dish, please?	Есть у вас что-нибудь вегетарианское? **Yest** *oo vass shtor-neeboot vegetariarn-skoya?*
I'd like... _____	Мне...,пожалуйста *Mnyeh...,puzharlooysta*
I'd like a kilo of apples, ___ please.	Мне килограмм яблок, пожалуйста *Mnyeh keelugrahm yabluk, puzharlooysta*
Can I...?_____	Можно...? *Morzhna...?*
Can I take this?_____	Можно это забрать? *Morzhna eta zubbrart?*
Can I smoke here?_____	Здесь можно курить? *Zdyess morzhno kooreet?*
Could I ask you _____ something?	Можно вас спросить? *Morzhno vass sprusseet?*

.3 How to reply

Yes, of course _____	Да, конечно *Dah, kunyeshna*
No, I'm sorry_____	Нет, извините *Nyet, eezvineetyeh*
Yes, what can I do _____ for you?	Да, что я могу для вас сделать? *Dah, shto yah muggoo dlya vass zdyellat?*
Just a moment, please ____	Одну минуту, пожалуйста *Udnoo minootoo, puzharlooysta*
No, I don't have _____ time now	Нет, мне некогда *Nyet, mnyeh nyaykugda*
No, that's impossible _____	Нет, это невозможно *Nyet, eta nivuzmorzhna*
I think so _____	Я думаю, да *Ya doomuyoo, dah*
I agree_____	Я тоже так думаю *Ya torzha tak doomuyoo*
I hope so too_____	Я тоже надеюсь *Ya torzha nudyeyus*
No, not at all _____	Нет, совсем нет **Nyet,** *suvsyem nyet*

No, no one _____	Нет, никто
	Nyet, neektor
No, nothing_____	Нет, ничего
	Nyet, nichivvor
That's (not) right _____	Это правильно (неправильно)
	Eto prarveelna (niprarveelna)
I (don't) agree _____	Я с вами (не) согласен
	Ya svarmee (nyeh) sugglarssin
All right _____	Хорошо
	Khurushor
Okay _____	Ладно
	Lardna
Perhaps _____	Может быть
	Morzhit byt
I don't know _____	Не знаю
	Nyeh znah-yu

.4 Thank you

Thank you _____	Спасибо
	Spaseeba
You're welcome _____	Не за что
	Nyeh za shto
Thank you very much _____	Огромное спасибо
	Ugrormnaya spaseeba
Very kind of you_____	Очень мило с вашей стороны
	Orchin meela svarshay sturrunny
I enjoyed it very much _____	Это доставило мне огромное удовольствие
	Eto dustarveelo mnyeh urgrormnaya ooduvvorlstviyeh
Thank you for your _____ trouble	Благодарю за беспокойство
	Bluggudurryoo za byespukkoystva
You shouldn't have _____	Не нужно было этого делать
	Nyeh noozhno byla etuvva dyelut
That's all right _____	Всё в порядке
	Vsyor fpuryatkyeh

.5 Sorry

Excuse me _____	Пардон
	Pardorn
Sorry! _____	Извините!
	Eezvineetyeh!
I'm sorry, I didn't know..._	Извините, я не знал (знала), что...
	Eezvineetyeh, ya nyeh znarl (znarla), shtor...
I do apologise_____	Простите меня
	Prusteetyeh minya
I'm sorry_____	Извините
	Eezvineetyeh
I didn't do it on purpose,___ it was an accident	Я не нарочно, это произошло случайно
	Ya nyeh nurrorchna, eta pra-eezushlor sluchayna
That's all right _____	Ничего страшного
	Nichivvor strarshnuvva

Never mind _____	Оставьте
	Ustarvtyeh
It could've happened to___ anyone	Со всяким может случиться
	Sa fsyarkim morzhit sloocheetsa

2.6 What do you think?

Which do you prefer?_____	Что вы предпочитаете?
	Shto vy pridpuchitah-yettyeh?
What do you think?_____	Что ты об этом думаешь?
	Shto ty ub etum doomuyesh?
Don't you like dancing? ___	Ты не любишь танцевать?
	Ty nyeh lyoobish tuntsivart?
I don't mind_____	Мне всё равно
	Mnyeh fsyo ruvnor
Well done! _____	Хорошо!
	Khurushor!
Not bad!_____	Неплохо!
	Niplorkha!
Great! _____	Великолепно!
	Vileekulyepna!
Wonderful! _____	Прекрасно!
	Prikrarsno!
It's really nice here! _____	Как здесь уютно!
	Kukk zdyess oo-yootna!
How nice! _____	Как здорово/красиво!
	Kukk zdoruvva/krusseeva!
How nice for you! _____	Как здорово для вас!
	Kukk zdoruvva dlya vass!
I'm (not) very happy_____ with...	Я (не) очень доволен (довольна) по поводу...
	Ya (nyeh) orchin duvorlyin/duvorlna puh porvuddoo...
I'm glad..._____	Я рад (рада), что...
	Ya raht (rarda), shtor...
I'm having a great time ____	Я прекрасно провожу время
	Ya prikrarsna pruvvuzhoo vraymya
I'm looking forward to it ___	Я заранее рад (рада)
	Ya zurarnyehyeh raht (rarda)
I hope it'll work out_____	Надеюсь, что это удастся
	Nudyay-yus, shtor eta oodarstsa
That's ridiculous! _____	Какая чушь!
	Kukkahya choosh!
That's terrible! _____	Как ужасно!
	Kukk oozharsno!
What a pity! _____	Как жаль!
	Kukk zharl!
That's filthy! _____	Как противно!
	Kukk prutteevna!
What a load of rubbish! ___	Какая ерунда!
	Kukkahya yiroondah!
I don't like..._____	Я не люблю...
	Ya nyeh lyooblyoo...
I'm bored to death _____	Я ужасно скучаю
	Ya oozharsno skoochahyoo

I've had enough	Мне надоело
	Mnye0h nuddayello
This is no good	Так нельзя
	Tukk nilzyah
I was expecting something completely different	Я ожидал (ожидала) совсем другого
	Ya uzhidarl (uzhidarla) sufsyem droogorva

Conversation

Conversation

3 .1 I beg your pardon?

I don't speak any/ I speak a little...	Я не говорю по-.../Я немного говорю п-... *Ya nyeh guvvuryoo puh.../Ya nimnorga guvvuryoo puh...*
I'm British	Я из Великобритании *Ya ees Vileekobritarnee-ee*
I'm English	Я англичанин/англичанка *Ya unglicharnin/unglicharnka*
I'm Scottish	Я шотландец/шотландка *Ya shutlarndyits/shutlarntka*
I'm Welsh	Я валлиец/валлийка *Ya vulleeyits/vulleeka*
I'm Irish	Я ирландец/ирландка *Ya irlarndits/irlarntka*
Do you speak English/French/German?	Вы говорите по-английски/по-французски/по-немецки? *Vy guvureetye puh-angleeski/puh-frantsooski/puh-nimyetski?*
Is there anyone who speaks...?	Кто-нибудь говорит по-...? *Ktor-neeboot guvureet puh...?*
I beg your pardon?	Что вы сказали? *Shtor vy skuzarli?*
I (don't) understand	Я (не) понимаю *Ya (nyeh) punnimahyu*
Do you understand me?	Вы меня понимаете? *Vy minya punnimahyetyeh?*
Could you repeat that, please?	Повторите, пожалуйста *Pufturreetyeh, puzharlooysta*
Could you speak more slowly, please?	Говорите медленнее, пожалуйста *Guvurreetyeh myaydlinyayeh, puzharlooysta*
What does that (word) mean?	Что это значит?/Что это слово означает? *Shtor eto znarchit? Shtor eto slorva uzznuchahyet?*
Is that similar to/the same as...?	Это (примерно) то же самое, как... ? *Eta (preemyairna) tor zheh sarmoyeh, kukk...?*
Could you write that down for me, please?	Напишите это для меня, пожалуйста *Nupisheetyeh eta dlya minya, puzharlooysta*
Could you spell that for me, please? **(See 1.8 Telephone alphabet)**	Скажите по буквам, пожалуйста *Skuzheetyeh pa bookvum, puzharlooysta*
Could you point that out in this phrase book, please?	Покажите в этой книжке, пожалуйста *Pukkuzheetye vetoy kneeshkye, puzharlooysta*
One moment, please, I have to look it up	Минуточку, мне нужно поискать *Meenootuchkoo, mnyeh noozhna puh-eeskart*
I can't find the word/the sentence	Я не могу найти это слово/предложение *Ya nyeh muggoo nigh-tee eto slorva/ pridd-dluzhayniyeh*
How do you say that in...?	Как это сказать по-...? *Kukk eta skuzzart puh...?*
How do you pronounce that?	Как это произносится? *Kukk eta pra-eeznorsitsa?*

May I introduce myself? ___ Разрешите представиться
Razrisheetyeh pridstarvitsa

My name's... _____ Меня зовут...
Minya zuvvoot...

I'm... _____ Я...
Ya...

What's your name? _____ Как вас зовут?
Kukk vas zuvvoot?

May I introduce...? _____ Можно вам представить?
Morzhna varm pridstarvit?

This is my wife/ _____ Это моя жена/дочь/мать/подруга
   daughter/mother/girlfriend *Eto muyah zhinnah/dorch/mart/puddrooga*

– my husband/son/ _____ Это мой муж/сын/отец/друг
   father/boyfriend *Eto moy moozh/syn/uttyets/drook*

How do you do _____ Здравствуйте, рад (рада) вас видеть
Zdrarstvooytyeh, raht (rarda) vas veedit

Pleased to meet you _____ Очень приятно (познакомиться)
Orchin priyartno (puznukormitsa)

Where are you from? _____ Откуда вы?
Utkooda vy?

I'm from _____ Я из Англии/Шотландии/Уэльса/Ирландии
   England/Scotland/Wales/ *Ya ees Arnglee-ee/Shutlarndee-ee/Oo-*
   Ireland *elsa/Eerlarndee-ee*

What city do you live in? ___ В каком городе вы живёте?
Fkukkorm gorudyeh vy zhyvyotyeh?

In..., it's near... _____ В...Это недалеко от...
V...Eto nidullikor ut...

Have you been here _____ Вы уже давно здесь?
   long? *Vy oozheh duvnor zdyess?*

A few days _____ Несколько дней
Nyeskulka dnyay

How long are you _____ Сколько вы здесь пробудете?
   staying here? *Skorlka vy zdyess praboodyetyeh?*

We're (probably) leaving ___ Мы уезжаем (скорее всего) завтра/через
   tomorrow/in two weeks две недели
My ooyizhahyem (skorayeh vsivvor) zarf-
tra/chayruss dvyeh nidyayli

Where are you staying? ____ Где вы остановились?
Gdyeh vy ustunnuveelis?

In a hotel/an apartment ____ В гостинице/квартире
Vgusteenitseh/kvarteeryeh

On a camp site _____ В кемпинге
Fkempingeh

With friends/relatives _____ У друзей/родственников
Oo droozyay/rortstvinneekuff

Are you here on your _____ Вы здесь один (одна)/с семьёй?
   own/with your family? *Vy zdyess udeen (udnah)/s simyoy?*

I'm on my own _____ я один (одна)
Ya udeen (udnah)

I'm with my _____ я с партнёром/женой/мужем
   partner/wife/husband *Ya spartnyorum/zhinoy/moozhum*

– with my family _____ я с семьёй
Ya s-simyoy

– with relatives _____ я с родственниками
Ya srortstvinneekummi

Conversation

– with a boy/girl friend/friends	я с другом/подругой/друзьями
	Ya zdroogum/spuddroogoy/zdroozyarmi
Are you married?	Вы женаты (замужем)?
	Vy zhinarty (zarmoozhum)?
Do you have a steady boyfriend/girlfriend?	У тебя есть постоянный друг? (У тебя есть постоянная подруга?)
	Oo tibyah yest pustuyahny drook? (Oo tibyah yest pustuyahnaya puddrooga?)
That's none of your business	Это вас не касается
	Eto vas nyeh kasah-yitsa
I'm married	Я женат (замужем)
	Ya zhinart (zarmoozhum)
– single	Я холостяк
	Ya khullustyark
– separated	Я живу отдельно
	Ya zhivoo utdyelna
– divorced	Я разведён (разведена)
	Ya ruzvidyon (ruzvidyinah)
– a widow/widower	Я вдова/вдовец
	Ya vduvvah/vduvvyets
I live alone/with someone	Я живу один (одна)/я живу совместно
	Ya zhivoo udeen (udnah)/Ya zhivoo suvvmyestna
Do you have any children/grandchildren?	У вас есть дети/внуки?
	Oo vas yest dyayti/vnooki?
How old are you?	Сколько вам лет?
	Skorlka varm lyet?
How old is she/he?	Сколько ей/ему лет?
	Skorlka yey/yimoo lyet?
I'm...	Мне...лет
	Mnyeh...lyet
She's/he's...	Ей/ему...лет
	Yey/yimoo...lyet
What do you do for a living?	Кем вы работаете?
	Kyem vy rubortayetyeh?
I work in an office	Я работаю в учреждении
	Ya rubortayu voochrizhdyaynii
I'm a student/ I'm at school	Я учусь/я учусь в школе
	Ya oochoos/Ya oochoos vshkorlyeh
I'm unemployed	Я безработный
	Ya byizrubortny
I'm retired	Я на пенсии
	Ya nah pyensii
I'm on a disability pension	Я признан неспособным к работе
	Ya preeznun nyespusorbnym krubortye
I'm a housewife	я домохозяйка
	Ya dummakhuzyayka
Do you like your job?	Вам нравится ваша работа?
	Varm nrarvitsa varsha rubborta?
Most of the time	Иногда да, иногда нет
	Eenugdah dah, eenugdah nyet
I usually do, but I prefer holidays	В основном да, но отпуск мне нравится больше
	Vusnuvnorm dah, noh ortpusk mnyeh nrarvitsa borlsheh

3.3 Starting/ending a conversation

Could I ask you _____ something?	Можно вас спросить? *Morzhna vas spruseet?*
Excuse me _____	Извините/Простите *Eezvineetyeh/Prusteetyeh*
Excuse me, could you ____ help me?	Извините, вы не могли бы помочь? *Eezvineetyeh, vy nyeh muglee by pumorch?*
Yes, what's the _____ problem?	Да, что случилось? *Dah, shtor sloocheeloss?*
What can I do for you? ____	Что я могу для вас сделать? *Shtor ya muggoo dlya vas zdyelat?*
Sorry, I don't have time ____ now	Простите, мне некогда *Prusteetyeh, mnyeh nyekugda*
Do you have a light? _____	Прикурить не найдётся? *Prikureet nyeh nigh-dyotsa?*
May I join you? _____	Можно сесть рядом с вами? *Morzhna syest ryardum svarmi?*
Could you take a _____ picture of me/us? Press this button	Вы не могли бы меня/нас сфотографировать? Нажмите эту кнопку *Vy nyeh mugglee by minya sfuttugrufeeruvat? Nuzhmeetyeh etoo knorpkoo*
Leave me alone _____	Оставь меня в покое *Ustarf minya fpukoyeh*
Get lost _____	Убирайся *Oobirigh-sya*
Go away or I'll scream ____	Если вы не отойдёте, я закричу *Yesli vy nyeh uttuydyotyeh, ya zukrichoo*

3.4 Congratulations and condolences

Happy birthday/Happy ____ name day	Поздравляю с днём рождения/Поздравляю с именинами *Puzdruvlyayu zdnyom ruzhdyayniya/ Puzdruvlyayu seemineenummi*
Please accept my _____ condolences	Мои соболезнования *Ma-ee subbulyeznuvarniya*
I'm very sorry for you ____	Я вам очень сочувствую *Ya varm orchin suchoostvooyu*

3 .5 A chat about the weather

See also 1.5 The weather

It's so hot/cold today!_____	Как сегодня тепло/холодно! *Kukk sivordnya tiplor/khorludna!*
Nice weather, isn't it?_____	Хорошая погода, не правда ли? *Khurorshaya puggorda, nyeh prarvda lee?*
What a wind/storm! _____	Какой ветер! Какая буря! *Kukkoy vayter! Kukkaya boorya!*
All that rain/snow! _____	Какой дождь/снег! *Kukkoy dorzht/snyek!*
All that fog!_____	Какой туман! *Kukkoy toomarn!*
Has the weather been _____ like this for long here?	Здесь уже давно такая погода? *Zdyess oozheh duvnor tukkaya puggorda?*
Is it always this hot/cold ___ here?	Здесь всегда так тепло/холодно? *Zdyess fsigdar tukk tiplor/khorludna?*
Is it always this dry/wet____ here?	Здесь всегда так сухо/сыро? *Zdyess fsigdar tukk sookha/syra?*

3 .6 Hobbies

Do you have any _____ hobbies?	У вас есть хобби? *Oo vas yest khorbi?*
I like knitting/ _____ reading/photography/ DIY	Я люблю вязать/читать/фотографировать/ мастерить *Ya lublyoo vyizart/chitart/futugrufeeru-vart/mustyereet*
I like music _____	Я люблю музыку *Ya lublyoo moozyku*
I like playing the _____ guitar/piano	Я люблю играть на гитаре/пианино *Ya lublyoo eegrart nah geetaryeh/pee-uneeno*
I like going to the _____ movies	Я люблю ходить в кино *Ya lublyoo khudeet fkeenor*
I like travelling/_____ sport/fishing/walking	Я люблю путешествовать/заниматься спортом/ловить рыбу/гулять *Ya lublyoo pootyishestvuvart/zunimartsa sportum/luveet ryboo/goolyart*

3 .7 Being the host(ess)

See also 4 Eating out

Can I offer you a drink? ____	Разрешите предложить вам чего-нибудь выпить? *Ruzrisheetyeh pridluzheet varm chivorniboot vypeet?*
What would you like_____ to drink?	Что ты будешь пить? *Shtor ty boodyesh peet?*
Something non-_____ alcoholic, please	Что-нибудь без алкоголя, пожалуйста *Shto-niboot byes ulkugorlya, puzharlooysta*

Would you like a _____ cigarette/cigar/Russian *papirorssa?*	Вы хотите сигарету/сигару/папиросу? *Vy khuteetye sigaryetoo/sigaroo/papirorssoo?*
I don't smoke _____	Я не курю *Ya nyeh kooryoo*

.8 Invitations

Are you doing anything ___ tonight?	Уы сегодня занят (занята)? *Ty sivordnya zarnyut (zanyutah)?*
Do you have any plans ____ for today/this afternoon/tonight?	У вас есть планы на сегодня/сегодня днём/сегодня вечером? *Oo vas yest plarny nah sivordnya/sivordnya dnyom/sivordnya vaychiram?*
Would you like to go _____ out with me?	Хотите провести время со мной? *Khuteetyeh pruvistee vraymya sumnoy?*
Would you like to go _____ dancing with me?	Хотите со мной потанцевать? *Khuteetyeh sumnoy putantsivart?*
Would you like to have ___ lunch/dinner with me?	Хотите вместе поужинать? *Khuteetyeh vmyestyeh pu-oozhinut?*
Would you like to come____ to the beach with me?	Хотите пойти со мной на пляж? *Khuteetyeh puytee sumnoy na plyahsh?*
Would you like to come____ into town with us?	Хотите пойти с нами в город? *Khuteetyeh puytee snarmi vgorut?*
Would you like to come____ and see some friends with us?	Хотите пойти с нами к друзьям? *Khuteetyeh puytee snarmi kdroozyarm?*
Shall we dance? _____	Потанцуем? *Putantsooyem?*
– sit at the bar? _____	Пойдём к бару? *Puydyom kbaroo?*
– get something to drink? __	Выпьем что-нибудь? *Vypyum shto-niboot?*
– go for a walk/drive? _____	Пойдём прогуляемся/покатаемся? *Puydyom prugoolyahyimsya/pukutahyimsya?*
Yes, all right _____	Да, хорошо *Dah, khurushor*
Good idea _____	Неплохая идея *Nyiplukhaya eedyaya*
No (thank you_____	Нет (спасибо) *Nyet (spaseeba)*
Maybe later _____	Может быть, попозже *Morzhit byt, puporzha*
I don't feel like it _____	У меня нет настроения *Oo minya nyet nustruyayniya*
I don't have time _____	У меня нет времени *Oo minya nyet vraymini*
I already have a date _____	Я уже договорился (договорилась) с другим *Ya oozheh dugguvvureelsya (dugguvvureelas) zdroogeem*
I'm not very good at_____ dancing/volleyball/ swimming	Я не умею танцевать/играть в волейбол/плавать *Ya nyeh oomyayu tantsivart/eegrart v vullayborl/plarvut*

3.9 Paying a compliment

You look wonderful!	Как вы хорошо выглядите!
	Kukk vy khurushor vyglyadeeteyeh!
I like your car!	Красивая машина!
	Kruseevaya musheena!
I like your ski outfit!	Замечательный лыжный костюм!
	Zamichartyelny lyzhny kustyoom!
You're a nice boy/girl	Ты милый мальчик/Ты милая девочка
	Ty meely marlchik/Ty meelaya dyevuchka
What a sweet child!	Какой милый ребёнок!
	Kukkoy meely ribyonuk!
You're a wonderful dancer!	Вы очень хорошо танцуете
	Vy orchin khurushor tantsooyetyeh
You're a wonderful cook!	Вы очень хорошо готовите
	Vy orchin khurushor gutorvityeh
You're a terrific soccer player!	Вы очень хорошо играете в футбол
	Vy orchin khurushor eegrahyetyeh v futborl

3.10 Chatting someone up

I like being with you	Мне с тобой очень приятно
	Mnyeh stuboy orchin priyartno
I've missed you so much	Я так по тебе скучал (скучала)
	Ya tak puh tibyeh skoocharl (skoocharla)
I dreamt about you	Ты мне снился (снилась)
	Ty mnyeh sneelsya (sneelas)
I think about you all day	Я целый день о тебе думаю
	Ya tsely dyen o tibyeh doomuyu
You have such a sweet smile	Ты так мило смеёшься
	Ty tukk meelo smeeyoshsya
You have such beautiful eyes	У тебя такие красивые глаза
	Oo tibya tukkeeya kruseevy-yeh gluzzah
I'm in love with you	Я в тебя влюблён (влюблена)
	Ya ftibya vlyublyon (vlyublinah)
I'm in love with you too	Я в тебя тоже
	Ya ftibya torzheh
I love you	Я тебя люблю
	Ya tibya lyublyoo
I love you too	Я тебя тоже
	Ya tibya torzheh
I don't feel as strongly about you	У меня не такие сильные чувства к тебе
	Oo minya nyeh tukkeeyeh seelny-yeh choostva ktibyeh
I already have a boyfriend/girlfriend	У меня уже есть друг/подруга
	Oo minya oozheh yest drook/puddrooga
I'm not ready for that	Я ещё к этому не готов (готова)
	Ya yishchor ketummoo nyeh gutorf (gutorva)
This is going too fast for me	Всё происходит слишком быстро
	Fsyor pru-eeskhordit sleeshkum bystra
Take your hands off me	Отстань
	Utstan
Okay, no problem	Ладно, ничего
	Lardna, nichivvor

Will you stay with me tonight?	Ты останешься у меня сегодня на ночь?
	Ty ustarnyeshsya oo minya sivordnya narnuch?
I'd like to go to bed with you	Я хочу с тобой спать
	Ya khuchoo stuboy spart
Only if we use a condom	Только с презервативом
	Torlko sprezairvateevum
We have to be careful about AIDS	Мы должны быть осторожны из-за СПИДа
	My dulzhny byt usturorzhny eez-zah speeda
That's what they all say	Все так говорят
	Vsyeh tukk guvuryat
We shouldn't take any risks	Не будем рисковать
	Nyeh boodyem reeskuvart
Do you have a condom?	У тебя есть презерватив?
	Oo tibya yest prezairvateef?
No? In that case we won't do it	Нет? Тогда не будем
	Nyet? Tudgah nyeh boodyum

❸.11 Arrangements

When will I see you again?	Когда я тебя снова увижу?
	Kugdah ya tibya snorvah ooveezhu?
Are you free over the weekend?	У вас есть время в выходные?
	Oo vas yest vraymya v vykhudny-yeh?
What shall we arrange?	Как мы договоримся?
	Kukk my dugguvvureemsya?
Where shall we meet?	Где мы встретимся?
	Gdyeh my fstraytimsya?
Will you pick me/us up?	Вы за мной/нами заедете?
	Vy za mnoy/narmi zayaydyetyeh?
Shall I pick you up?	Давайте я за вами заеду
	Duv-igh-tyeh ya za varmi zayaydu
I have to be home by...	Я должен (должна) быть дома в...часов
	Ya dorlzhen (dulzhnah) byt dorma v... chussorf
I don't want to see you anymore	Я вас больше не хочу видеть
	Ya vas borlshe nyeh khuchoo veedyet
Can I take you home?	Могу ли я отвезти вас домой?
	Muggoo lee ya utvistee vas dumoy?

❸.12 Saying goodbye

Can I write/call you?	Я вам могу написать/позвонить?
	Ya vam muggoo napisart/puzvuneet?
Will you write/call me?	Вы мне напишете/позвоните?
	Vy mnyeh napeeshutyeh/puzvuneetyeh?
Can I have your address/phone number?	Можно ваш адрес/телефон?
	Morzhno varsh ardris/tyeleforn?
Thanks for everything	Спасибо за всё
	Spaseeba za fsyoh
It was very nice	Было замечательно
	Byla zamichartelna
Say hello to...	Передай привет...
	Pirid-igh preevyet...
All the best	Всего самого лучшего
	Fsivor sarmuva loochshiva

Good luck _____	Дальнейших успехов
	Dalnyayshikh oospyekhoff
When will you be back? ___	Когда ты снова придёшь?
	Kugdah ty snorva preedyosh?
I'll be waiting for you _____	Я буду тебя ждать
	Ya boodoo tibya zhdart
I'd like to see you again____	Я бы хотел (хотела) увидеть тебя ещё раз
	Ya by khutyel (khutyela) ooveedit tibya yishchor rarss
I hope we meet _____ again soon	Надеюсь, что мы скоро друг друга снова увидим
	Nudyayus, shtor my skora drook drooga ooveedim
This is our address, _____ if you're ever in the UK	Вот наш адрес, если вы когда-нибудь будете в Великобритании/Англии...
	Vort narsh ardris, yesli vy kugdah-niboot boodyutyeh v Veleekobritarnii/Arnglii...
You'd be more than _____ welcome	Будем рады вас видеть
	Boodyem rardy vas veedit

4

Eating out

4 Eating out

● **In Russia** hotel restaurants usually provide three meals. Breakfast (завтрак, *zarftrak*) is between 8.00am and 10.00am and may offer juice, yoghurt, omelette, bread, butter, sausage or other meats, cheese, jam, cereal, tea and coffee. Lunch (обед, *ubyet*) is the main meal and is served between 12.00 and 1.30pm. It has at least three courses. The first is закуски, *zakooski* (starters, appetizers), which might be an egg dish, sliced meat or sausage, pickled cucumbers, fish, mushrooms, salads, brawn, or caviar. The soups often served after the *zakooski* can be a meal in themselves. The main course is meat, fish or game with some potatoes and vegetables (the latter are not as important as in British cooking). The sweet course might be pancakes, stewed fruit, a tart, or ice cream. The evening meal (ужин, *oozhin*) is from 7.00pm to 10.00pm. It is generally a lighter version of *ubyet* and may be no more than various kinds of open sandwiches with tea and coffee.

4 .1 On arrival

I'd like to book a table _____ for seven o'clock, please	Можно заказать стол на семь часов? *Morzhna zukkuzzart storl nah syem chassorf?*
I'd like a table for two, _____ please	Пожалуйста, столик на двоих *Puzharlooysta, storlik nah dvu-eekh*
We've/we haven't booked __	Мы (не) заказывали *My (nyeh) zukkarzyvarli*
Is the restaurant open _____ yet?	Кухня уже открыта? *Kookhnya oozheh utkryta?*
What time does the _____ restaurant open/close?	Когда кухня открывается/закрывается? *Kugdar kookhnya utkryvayetsya/zukkryvayetsya?*
Can we wait for a table? ___	Мы можем подождать столик? *My morzhum pudduzhdart storlik?*
Do we have to wait long? __	Нам придётся долго ждать? *Narm preedyotsya dorlga zhdart?*
Is this seat taken? _____	Это место свободно? *Eta myesta svubbordna?*
Could we sit here/there? ___	Можно здесь/там сесть? *Morzhna zdyess/tarm syest?*
Can we sit by the_____ window?	Можно сесть у окна? *Morzhna syest oo ukknar?*
Can we eat outside? _____	Можно есть во дворе/на воздухе? *Morzhna yest vudvurryeh/nah vorz-dookhyeh?*

Вы заказывали? _____	Do you have a reservation?
На какую фамилию? _____	What name, please?
Сюда, пожалуйста _____	This way, please
Этот стол заказан _____	This table is reserved
Через пятнадцать минут _____ столик освободится	We'll have a table free in fifteen minutes
Вы не могли бы подождать у бара? _____	Would you like to wait (at the bar)?

Do you have another _____ chair for us?	Принесите нам ещё один стул, пожалуйста
	Preenisseetyeh nahm yishchor udeen stool, puzharlooysta
Do you have a highchair? ___	Принесите нам ещё детский стул, пожалуйста
	Preenisseetyeh nahm yishchor dyetski stool, puzharlooysta
Is there a socket for _____ this bottle-warmer?	Есть ли для этого нагревателя бутылочки розетка?
	Yest lee dlya etuvva nuggrivartyelya bootyluchki ruzzyetka?
Could you warm up _____ this bottle/jar for me?	Вы можете разогреть для меня эту бутылочку/баночку?
	Vy morzhityeh ruzzugryayt dlya minya etoo bootyluchkoo/ barnuchkoo?
Not too hot, please _____	Не очень горячо, пожалуйста
	Nyeh orchin guryachor, puzharlooysta
Is there somewhere I _____ can change the baby's nappy?	У вас есть помещение, где я могу переодеть ребёнка?
	Oo vas yest pummishchayneeyeh, gdyeh ya muggoo pirreeuddyayt ribbyonka?
Where are the toilets? _____	Где туалет?
	Gdyeh too-ullyet?

Eating out

🔵.2 Ordering

Waiter! _____	Официант!
	Uffitsiant!
Madam! _____	Госпожа!
	Guspuzhar!
Sir!_____	Господин!
	Guspuddeen!
We'd like something to ___ eat/a drink	Мы хотели бы поесть/попить
	My khuttyayli by puyest/puppeet
Could I have a quick_____ meal?	Могу я быстро поесть?
	Muggoo ya bystra puyest?
We don't have much time__	У нас мало времени
	Oo nuss marla vrayminee
We'd like to have a _____ drink first	Мы сначала хотели бы чего-нибудь попить
	My snucharla khuttyayli by chivvor-niboot puppeet
Could we see the_____ menu/wine list, please?	Принесите нам меню/меню спиртных напитков, пожалуйста
	Preenisseetyeh nahm minyoo/minyoo spirtnykh nuppeetkuff, puzharlooysta
Do you have a menu _____ in English?	У вас есть меню на английском?
	Oo vas yest minyoo na angleeskum?
Do you have a dish_____ of the day?/Tourist menu?	У вас есть суточное меню?/У вас есть туристское меню?
	Oo vas yest sootuchnoyeh minyoo?/Oo vas yest tooreestskoyeh minyoo?
We haven't made a_____ choice yet	Мы ещё не выбрали
	My yishchor nyeh vybrulli
What do you _____ recommend?	Что бы вы порекомендовали?
	***Shtor** by vy purrekumminduvvarli?*

What are the specialities of the region/the house?	Какие фирменные блюда этой области/этого ресторана?
	Kukkeeyeh feermyenny-yeh blyooda etoy orblasti/etuvva resturrarna?
I like strawberries/olives	Я люблю клубнику/оливки
	Ya lyublyoo kloobneekoo/ulleefki
I don't like fish/meat...	Я не люблю рыбу/мясо/ ...
	Ya nyeh lyublyoo ryboo/myarsa
What's this?	Что это?
	Shtor eta?
Does it have...in it?	Сюда входят...?
	Syudar vkhordyut...?
Is this a hot or a cold dish?	Это горячее или холодное блюдо?
	Eto guryarchiyeh eeli khullordnuyeh blyooda?
Is this sweet?	Это сладкое блюдо?
	Eto slartkoyeh blyooda?
Is this spicy?	Это пикантное/острое блюдо?
	Eto peekarntnuyeh/orstruyeh blyooda?
Do you have anything else, please?	У вас нет ничего другого?
	Oo vas nyet nichivvor droogorva?
I'm on a salt-free diet	Мне нельзя солёного
	Mnyeh nilzyah sullyonuvva
I can't eat pork	Мне нельзя свинины
	Mnyeh nilzyah sveeneeny
– sugar	Мне нельзя сладкого
	Mnyeh nilzyah slartkuvva
– fatty foods	Мне нельзя жирного
	Mnyeh nilzyah zheernuvva
– (hot) spices	Мне нельзя острого
	Mnyeh nilzyah orstruvva
I'm not allowed alcohol	Мне нельзя пить
	Mnyeh nilzyah peet
I'll/we'll have what those people are having	То же, что и те люди заказали, пожалуйста
	Tor zheh, shtor ee tyeh lyoodyi zukkuzzarli, puzharlooysta
I'd like...	Я бы хотел (хотела)...
	Ya by knuttyel (khuttyela)...
We're not having a starter	Закуска нам не нужна
	Zukkooska num nyeh noozhnah

Вы хотите поесть?	Would you like a drink first?
Вы выбрали?	Have you decided?
Что вы хотите пить?	What would you like to drink?
Приятного аппетита.	Enjoy your meal
Вы хотите десерт/кофе/чай?	Would you like a dessert/coffee/tea?

The child will share _____ what we're having	Ребёнок поест что-нибудь из наших тарелок
	Ribyonuk pu-yest shtor-niboot eess narshikh taryelukk
Could I have some _____ more bread, please?	Ещё хлеба, пожалуйста
	Yishchor khlyeba, puzharlooysta
– a bottle of water/wine/ ___ vodka please?	Ещё бутылку воды/вина/водки, пожалуйста
	Yishchor bootylku vuddy/veenah/vortki, puzharlooysta
– another helping of... _____	Ещё порцию...
	Yishchor portseeyu...
– some salt and pepper ____	Принесите, пожалуйста, соль и перец
	Prinisseetyeh, puzharlooysta, sorl ee pyayrits
– a napkin _____	Принесите, пожалуйста, салфетку
	Prinisseetyeh, puzharlooysta, sulfyetkoo
– a spoon _____	Принесите, пожалуйста, ложечку
	Prinisseetyeh, puzharlooysta, lorzhuchkoo
– an ashtray _____	Принесите, пожалуйста, пепельницу
	Prinisseetyeh, puzharlooysta, paypyelnitsoo
– some matches _____	Принесите, пожалуйста, спички
	Prinisseetyeh, puzharlooysta, speechki
– some toothpicks _____	Принесите, пожалуйста, зубочистки
	Prinisseetyeh, puzharlooysta, zoobucheestki
– a glass of water _____	Принесите, пожалуйста, стакан воды
	Prinisseetyeh, puzharlooysta, stukkarn vuddy
– a straw (for the child) ___	Принесите, пожалуйста, соломинку (для ребёнка)
	Prinisseetyeh, puzharlooysta, sulormeenku (dlyah ribyonka)
Enjoy your meal! _____	Приятного аппетита!
	Preeyartnuvva appeteeta!
You too! _____	Того же
	Tuvvor zhe
Cheers! _____	(За) ваше здоровье!
	(Zah) varsha zdurorvyeh!
The next round's _____ on me	В следующий раз я плачу
	Fslyedooyushchee rass ya pluchoo

4.3 The bill

See also 8.2 Settling the bill

How much is this dish? ____	Сколько стоит это блюдо?
	Skorlka stor-eet eto blyooda?
Could I have the bill, _____ please?	Счёт, пожалуйста
	Shchot, puzharlooysta
All together _____	Всё вместе
	Fsyo vmyestyeh
Everyone pays separately__	Каждый платит за себя
	Karzhdy plartit za sibya
Could we have the menu __ again, please?	Можно ещё раз посмотреть меню?
	Morzhna yishchor rass pusmutrayt minyoo?
The...is not on the bill _____	...не занесено в счёт
	...nyeh zunnissinor fshchot

4 .4 Complaints

It's taking a very_____ long time	Это очень долго длится *Eto orchin dorlga dleetsya*
We've been here an _____ hour already	Мы сидим здесь уже час *My sideem zdyess oozheh charss*
This must be a mistake ____	Это, должно быть, ошибка *Eto, dulzhnor byt, ushypka*
This is not what I_____ ordered	Это не то, что я заказывал (заказывала) *Eto nyeh tor, shto ya zukkarzyval (zukkarzyvala)*
I ordered... _____	Я попросил (попросила)... *Ya pupprusseel (pupprusseela)...*
There's a dish missing ____	Одного блюда не хватает *Udnuvvor blyooda nyeh khvutigh-yet*
This is broken/not clean ___	Это сломано/грязно *Eto slormunna/gryahzna*
The food's cold _____	Еда холодная *Yiddah khulordnaya*
– not fresh _____	Еда несвежая *Yiddah nisvayzhaya*
– too salty/sweet/spicy_____	Еда слишком солёная/сладкая/острая *Yiddah sleeshkum sulyonaya/slartkaya/orstraya*
The meat's not done_____	Мясо не прожарилось *Myarsa nyeh pruzhareeluss*
– overdone _____	Мясо пережарено *Myarsa pirreezharina*
– tough _____	Мясо жёсткое *Myarsa zhostkaya*
– off _____	Мясо несвежее *Myarsa nisvayzhaya*
Could I have something ___ else instead of this?	Дайте мне вместо этого что-нибудь другое, пожалуйста *Digh-tye mnyeh vmyesta etuvva shtorniboot droogor-yeh, puzharlooysta*
The bill/this amount is _____ not right	По-моему, здесь неправильно *Puh-moyemoo zdyess nyeprarveelna*
We didn't have this_____	У нас этого не было *Oo nuss etuvva nyeh bylo*
There's no paper in the ____ toilet	В туалете нет бумаги *Ftooalyetyeh nyet boomargi*
Do you have a _____ complaints book?	У вас есть книга жалоб? *Oo vuss yest kneega zharlupp?*
Will you call the_____ manager, please?	Позовите, пожалуйста, начальника *Puzzuveetyeh, puzharlooysta, nacharlnika*

4 .5 Paying a compliment

That was a wonderful _____ meal	Мы прекрасно поели *My prikrarsna pu-yayli*
The food was excellent ____	Всё было очень вкусно *Fsyo byla orchin fkoosna*
The...in particular was ____ delicious	Особенно...был исключительным *Usorbinna...byl eesklyucheetyelnym*

4.6 The menu

безалкогольные напитки non-alcoholic drinks	кофе coffee	спиртные/алкогольные напитки spirits/alcoholic drinks
вина wines	мясо meat	супы soups
вторые блюда main course	национальные блюда national dishes	ужин dinner/evening meal
горячие супы hot soups	обед lunch	фирменные блюда specialities of the house
десерт dessert	овощи vegetables	фрукты fruit
дичь game	первые блюда first courses	холодные супы cold soups
закуски starters	птица poultry	чай tea
завтрак breakfast	салаты salads	
	соки juices	

4.7 Alphabetical list of drinks and dishes

абрикос apricot	борщ borshch (beetroot soup)	ветчина, с ветчиной raw ham, with ham
ананас pineapple	бренди brandy	вино (белое, красное, сухое, сладкое) wine (white, red, dry, sweet)
антрекот rib steak	брынза ewe's milk cheese	виноград grapes
апельсин, апельсиновый orange	буженина boiled pork	виски (со льдом) whisky (on the rocks)
арбуз water-melon	булочка bread roll	вишни, вишнёвый cherries, cherry (adj.)
ассорти мясное/рыбное meat platter/fish platter	бульон clear soup	вырезка fillet
баклажаны, из баклажанов aubergines	бутерброд open sandwich	гарнир, с гарниром garnish, with trimmings
банан banana	вальдшнеп woodcock	говядина beef
баранина, из баранины mutton	вареники dumplings	горох, гороховый peas, from peas
бефстроганов beef stroganov	варёный (-ая, -ое) cooked	горчица mustard
бифштекс rumpsteak	варенье, с вареньем preserves, with preserves	гранат, гранатовый pomegranate, from pomegranate
блины/блинчики pancakes	ватрушка curd cheese bun	грейпфрут, грейпфрутовый grapefruit, from grapefruit
бобы beans	вермишель vermicelli	
	вермут vermouth	

41

грибной (-ое, -ая)/из
  грибов
from mushrooms/
  fungi
грибы, с грибами
mushrooms/fungi
груша
pear
гуляш
goulash
гусь
goose
джем
jam
джин (с тоником)
gin (and tonic)
дыня
honeydew melon
ёрш
ruff (freshwater fish)/
  mixture of vodka
  and beer (or wine)
жареный (-ая, -ое)
roasted/fried/grilled/
  broiled
желе
jelly/aspic
жюльен
stew
заливной (-ая, -ое)
jellied/in aspic
заяц
hare
изюм
raisins
икра (красная,
  чёрная)
caviar (red, black)
индейка
turkey
кабачки
courgettes
камбала
plaice
капуста, с капустой
cabbage, with
  cabbage
капуста (кислая,
  красная, цветная)
cabbage (sauerkraut,
  red cabbage,
  cauliflower)
карась, карп
carp
картофель
potatoes

каша
buckwheat
квас
kvass
кефир
buttermilk
кильки
sprats
клубника
strawberries
клюква,
  клюквенный
cranberry, from
  cranberries
колбаса
sausage
компот
stewed fruit
коньяк
cognac
копчёный
smoked
котлеты
Russian meatballs
котлеты по-киевски
chicken kiev
кофе (чёрный)
coffee (black)
краб, из крабов
crab, from crab
креветки
prawns
кролик
rabbit
кукуруза
maize
курица, с курицей
chicken, with
  chicken
куриный, из кур
from chicken
куропатка
partridge
лангет
roast sirloin
лапша
noodles/noodle
  soup
лещ
bream
ликёр
liqueur
лимон, с лимоном
lemon, with lemon
лимонад
lemonade

лососина/лосось
salmon
лук, с луком
onion, with onion
майонез, под
  майонезом
mayonnaise
макароны
macaroni
макрель
mackerel
мандарин,
  мандариновый
mandarin orange,
  from mandarins
маринованный (-ая,
  -ое)
pickled
маслины
black olives
мясо, мясной
meat, from meat
начинка, с начинкой
filling/with filling
овощи, овощной (-ая, -ое)
vegetables,
  vegetable (adj.)
огурец, из огурцов
ridge cucumber,
  made from ridge
  cucumbers
окорок
boiled ham
окрошка
cold soup with
  kvass, meat and
  vegetables
окунь
perch
оладьи
fritters
оливки
green olives
орехи
nuts
осётр/осетрина
sturgeon
отбивная
  котлета
chop
отварной (-ая, ое)
boiled/poached
палтус
halibut
• паровой (-ая, ое)
steamed

паштет
pâté
пельмени
dumplings filled with
  meat
перепел
quail
петрушка
parsley
печёнка
liver
печёный (-ая, ое)
baked
печенье
a cake/biscuit
пиво
beer
пирог/пирожок
pie
пирожное
pastries
пити
mutton soup
плов
pilaff
поджарка
grilled meat
помидоры, из
  помидоров
tomatoes, from
  tomatoes
пончик
deep-fried little pie
порей
leek
поросёнок/
  поросята
sucking pig
портвейн
port
похлёбка
thin soup
почки
kidneys
простокваша
yoghurt
пряник
spice cake
пудинг
pudding
пунш
punch
пюре
purée
рагу
ragout

рак
crayfish
рассольник
soup with pickled
  cucumbers
расстегай
small fish pie
редис(ка), из редиски
radish, from radishes
репа
turnip
рис, рисовый
rice
ром
rum
ростбиф
roast beef
рыбный (-ая, ое)
fish
рябчик
hazel grouse
ряженка
yoghurt made with
  evaporated milk
салат
salad
сардины
sardines
сахар, без сахара, с
  сахаром
sugar, without sugar,
  with sugar
свёкла
beetroot
свекольник
iced beetroot soup
свинина, из свинины
port
селёдка/сельдь
herring
сёмга
salmon
слива/со сливами
plum/with plums
сливовый
plum (adj.)
сливки (взбитые), со
  сливками
cream (whipped),
  with cream
сметана, со
  сметаной, в
  сметане
sour cream, with sour
  cream, in sour
  cream

смородина
currants
солёный (-ая, ое)
salted
солонина
salted beef
соль
salt
сом
catfish
сосиски/сардельки
frankfurter
  sausages/bangers
соус, под белым
  соусом
sauce, in white
  sauce
спаржа, спаржевый
asparagus
студень
fish in aspic/brawn
судак
zander
суп
soup
сыр
cheese
сырники
curd cheese fritters
сырок
curds pressed into a
  cheese shape
творог, с творогом
cottage cheese, with
  cottage cheese
телятина
veal
тефтели
meatballs
топлёное молоко
evaporated milk
торт
large many-layered
  cake
треска
cod
тресковая печень
cod-liver
тунец
tuna
тушёный (-ая, ое)
braised
тыква
pumpkin
угорь
eel

уксус
vinegar
устрицы
oysters
утка
duck
уха
fish soup
фаршированный
(-ая, ое)
stuffed
фасоль
beans
филе
fillet
финики
dates
форель
trout
фрукты, фруктовый
fruit
харчо
mutton soup with
  rice
херес
sherry
хлеб (белый,
  чёрный)
bread (white, black)
хрен, с хреном
horseradish, with
  horseradish

цыплёнок/цыплята
pullet/pullets
цыплёнок табака
Georgian boned
  chicken
чай
tea
чахохбили из кур
Caucasian chicken
  meatballs
чебуреки
Caucasian deep-fried
  stuffed dumplings
черемша
Caucasian wild onion
черешня
cherries
черника
 bilberry
чеснок, с чесноком
garlic, with garlic
шампанское (сухое,
  полусладкое,
  сладкое)
champagne (dry,
  demi-sec, sweet)
шашлык
shishkebab
шницель
schnitzel
шоколад, шоколадный
chocolate

шпинат
spinach
шпроты
sprats
щи
cabbage soup
щи кислые
sauerkraut soup
щи зелёные с яйцом
sorrel soup with
  beaten egg
эскалоп
cutlet
яблоко, с яблоками
apple, with apples
яблоко в тесте
apple pie
яблочный
apple (adj.)
язык
tongue
яйцо (всмятку,
  вкрутую)
egg (soft-boiled,
  hard-boiled)
яичница
fried egg

On the road

5 On the road

5.1 Asking for directions

Excuse me, could I ask you something?	Извините, можно вас спросить?
	Eezvineetyeh, morzhna vuss sprusseet?
I've lost my way	Я заблудился (заблудилась)
	Ya zubloodeelsya (zubloodeelas)
Is there a(n)... around here?	Вы не знаете, здесь поблизости...?
	Vy nyeh znah-yetyeh, zdyess publeezusti...?
Is this the way to...?	Это дорога в...?
	Eto durrorga v...?
Could you tell me how to get to the... (name of place)by car/on foot?	Вы не подскажете, как доехать/ дойти до...?
	Vy nyeh pudskarzhityeh, kukk duh-yekhat/duytee dor...?
What's the quickest way to...?	Как можно быстрее доехать до...?
	Kukk morzhna bystrayeh duh-yekhat dor...?
How many kilometres is it to...?	Сколько километров до...?
	Skorlka keelumyetruff dor...?
Could you point it out on the map?	Покажите на карте, пожалуйста
	Pukkuzheetyeh nah kartyeh, puzharlooysta

Я не знаю, я не отсюда	I don't know my way around here
Вы едете в неправильном направлении	You're going the wrong way
Вам нужно вернуться в...	You have to go back to...
Вы увидите, там будет написано	From there on just follow the signs
Там вам придётся снова спросить	When you get there, ask again

---

прямо	улица	река
straight ahead	the street	the river
налево	светофор	путепровод
left	the traffic lights	the flyover
направо	туннель	мост
right	the tunnel	the bridge
повернуть	знак "уступите дорогу"	железнодорожный переезд/шлагбаум
turn	the 'give way' sign	level crossing/ barrier
последовать		указатель направления...
follow	здание	
перейти	the building	the sign pointing to...
cross	на углу	стрелка
перекрёсток	at the corner	the arrow
the intersection		

● **Tourists wishing** to visit the Russian Federation must have a passport that is valid for the entire period that they will be in the country, and they must have a visa that is also valid for the specific period of their stay. Visas for visits that are arranged by tour companies are usually obtained by the company. Children who are included in the passport of one of the parents are added to the visa of that parent.

Visa application forms can be obtained from the Consulate General of the Russian Federation in London, 5 Kensington Palace Gardens, London W8 4QS, tel. 0171 229 8027, or the Consulate General in Edinburgh, 58 Melville Street, Edinburgh EG3 7HL, tel. 0131 225 7098. If you are going to Russia for a period of more than 3 months you must present a valid AIDS certificate.

At the border you must sign a customs declaration in which you state how much money you are carrying. A similar declaration is to be signed when you leave the country, There is no limit to the amount of foreign money and travellers' cheques you can take into Russia, but Russian money cannot be imported or exported and works of art/antiques may not be taken out without a licence.

Ваш паспорт, пожалуйста _____	Your passport, please
Ваша декларация, пожалуйста _____	Your customs declaration, please
Технический паспорт, пожалуйста_____	Your vehicle documents, please
Ваша виза, пожалуйста _____	Your visa, please
Куда вы едете?_____	Where are you heading?
Сколько вы собираетесь пробыть?____	How long are you planning to stay?
Есть ли у вас что-нибудь,_____ подлежащее оплате пошлиной?	Do you have anything to declare?
Откройте это, пожалуйста_____	Open this, please

My children are entered ___ on this passport	Мои дети вписаны в этот паспорт *Ma-ee dyayti fpeesunny vetut parsport*
I'm travelling through _____	Я проездом *Ya pru-yezdum*
I'm going on holiday to... __	Я еду в отпуск в... *Ya yay-doo vortpoosk v..*
I'm on a business trip _____	У меня деловая поездка *Oo minya dyeluvvaya pu-yestka*
I don't know how long_____ I'll be staying yet	Я ещё не знаю, сколько я пробуду *Ya yishchor nyeh znah-yu, skorlka ya pruboodoo*

I'll be staying here for _____ a weekend	Я на выходные
	Ya nah vykhudny-yeh
– for a few days _____	Я на несколько дней
	Ya nah nyeskulka dnyay
– for a week_____	Я на неделю
	Ya nah nidyaylyu
–for two weeks_____	Я на две недели
	Ya nah dvyeh nidyayli
I've got nothing to_____ declare	У меня нет ничего, что подлежит оплате пошлиной
	Oo minya nyet nichivvor, shto pudlizhyt uplartye porshlinoy
I've got...with me_____	У меня с собой есть...
	Oo minya s suboy yest...
– ...cartons of cigarettes ___	У меня с собой есть блок сигарет
	Oo minya s suboy yest blork seegurryet
– ...bottles of... _____	У меня с собой есть бутылки...
	Oo minya s suboy yest bootylki...
– some souvenirs _____	У меня с собой есть несколько сувениров
	Oo minya s suboy yest nyeskulka soovineeruff
These are personal _____ effects	Это личные вещи
	Eto leechny-yeh vyayshchi
These are not new _____	Эти вещи не новые
	Eti vyayshchi nyeh norvy-yeh
Here's the receipt _____	Вот чек
	Vort chyek
This is for private use ____	Это для меня
	Eto dlya minya
How much import duty ___ do I have to pay?	Сколько нужно заплатить за ввоз?
	Skorlka noozhna zuplutteet za v-vorz?
Can I go now? _____	Можно пройти?
	Morzhno pruytee?

🕔 .3 Luggage

Porter! _____	Носильщик!
	Nusseelshchik!
Could you take this_____ luggage to...?	Отнесите багаж в...,пожалуйста
	Utnisseetyeh buggarsh v...,puzharlooysta
How much do I_____ owe you?	Сколько с меня?
	Skorlka s minya?
Where can I find a_____ luggage trolley?	Где тележки для багажа?
	Gdyeh tilyeshki dlya bugguzhar?
Could you store this _____ luggage for me?	Могу я сдать багаж на хранение?
	Muggoo ya zdart buggarsh na khrunyayniya?
Where are the luggage ___ lockers?	Где автоматическая камера хранения?
	Gdyeh aftummuteecheskaya karmyera khrunyayniya?
I can't get the locker _____ open	Сейф не открывается
	Sayf nyeh unkryvahyetsya
How much is it per item ___ per day?	Сколько стоит сейф в день?
	Skorlko stor-it sayf v dyen?

This is not my bag/_____ suitcase	Это не моя сумка/Это не мой чемодан
	Eto nyeh muyah soomka/Eto nyeh moy chimmuddarn
There's one item/bag/ _____ suitcase missing still	Не хватает ещё одной вещи/сумки/не хватает ещё одного чемодана
	Nyeh khvuttah-yet yishchor udnoy vyayshchi/soomki/nyeh khvuttah-yet yish-chor udnuvvor chimmuddarna
My suitcase is damaged __	Мой чемодан повреждён
	Moy chimmuddarn puvrizhdyon

.4 Traffic signs

Russia uses the international traffic signs, but there are two special forms:

means STOP   *means END OF RESTRICTION*

You may also come across the following notices when driving:

Берегитесь автомобиля!	держитесь правой стороны	остановка запрещена
Watch out for cars	keep to the right	no stopping
велосипедисты	камнепад	переход
cyclists	falling rocks	crossing
внимание, впереди ведутся работы	обгон запрещён	плохая дорога
road works ahead	no overtaking	bad surface
(внимание)	обочина	светофор через сто метров
пешеходы	kerb	lights ahead 100 metres
Watch out for pedestrians	объезд	стоп
встречное движение	diversion	stop
oncoming traffic	ограничение скорости	стоянка запрещена
въезд запрещён	speed limit	no parking
no entry	одностороннее движение	сужение дороги
ГАИ	one-way traffic	road narrows
traffic police	опасно	такси
движение в один ряд	dangerous	taxi
	опасный поворот	таможня
single-file traffic	dangerous bend	Customs
	остановка автобуса	
	bus stop	

5.5 The car

See the diagram on page 53.

● **It is compulsory** for tourists motoring in Russia to have a valid international driving permit and carry first aid kit, fire extinguishers, a warning triangle, and a headlamp/beam converter. (For up-to-the-minute details ring AA Information, Overseas Travel, on 0990-500600.) It is also recommended to take with you at least spare fan-belts, bulbs and plugs.

Driving is on the right. Avoid night-driving. Seat-belts are compulsory for the driver and front-seat passenger. Fines are usually on the spot. The speed limit is 37 mph (60 km/h) in built-up areas, 55 mph (88 km/h) outside, and 43 mph (68 km/h) everywhere for motorists with less than 2 years' driving experience except where a lower limit is already indicated.

Personal safety. Before planning any visit to Russia at the moment it is imperative to contact the Foreign and Commonwealth Office Travel Advice Bureau, tel. 0171-238 4503.

5.6 The petrol station

● **Petrol in Russia** is often in short supply and filling stations few and far between. It is advisable to take reserve petrol in a can (import duty is payable on this). Petrol coupons can be bought with hard currency at the border and foreign currency is preferred when buying petrol. Unleaded petrol is not generally available. The most common diesel fuel is Солярка (*Solyar*ka).

How many kilometres to ___ the next petrol station, please?	Сколько километров до следующей заправочной станции? *Skor*lka keelumm**yet**ruff duss**lay**-dooyushchi zupp**rar**vochnoy starntsii?
I would like...litres of..., ___ please	Мне нужно...литров *Mnyeh n***oo**zhna...*leet*ruff
– petrol _____	Мне нужно...литров бензина *Mnyeh n***oo**zhna ... *leet*ruff ben**zee**na
– super _____	Мне нужно...литров бензина высшего качества *Mnyeh n***oo**zhna...*leet*ruff ben**zee**na vyss-shiva *kar*chistva
– diesel _____	Мне нужно...литров дизеля *Mnyeh n***oo**zhna...*leet*ruff d**ee**zilya
I would like...roubles' _____ worth of petrol, please	Мне нужен бензин за...рублей *Mnyeh n***oo**zhun ben**zeen** zah...**roob***lyay*
Fill her up, please _____	Полный бак, пожалуйста *Por*lny bark, puzh**ar***looysta*

Could you check...? _____	Проверьте, пожалуйста...
	Pruvyairtye, puzharlooysta...
– the oil level _____	Проверьте, пожалуйста, уровень масла
	Pruvyairtye, puzharlooysta, ooruvvin marssla
– the tyre pressure _____	Проверьте, пожалуйста, накачку шин
	Pruvyairtye, puzharlooysta, nukkarchkoo shin
Could you change the _____ oil, please?	Поменяйте масло, пожалуйста
	Puminyigh-tyeh marsslo, puzharlooysta
Could you clean the _____ windows/the windscreen, please?	Вымойте стёкла/ветровое стекло, пожалуйста
	Vymoytyeh styokla/vitruvoyeh stiklor, puzharlooysta
Could you give the car_____ a wash, please?	Помойте машину, пожалуйста
	Pumoytyeh mushinu, puzharlooysta

⑤ .7 Breakdown and repairs

I'm having car trouble._____ Could you give me a hand?	У меня авария. Вы можете мне помочь?
	Oo minya uvvariya. Vy morzhityeh mnyeh pummorch?
I've run out of petrol _____	У меня кончился бензин
	Oo minya korncheelsya binzeen
I've locked the keys_____ in the car	Я оставил(а) ключи в машине
	Ya ostarveel(a) klyoochee vmushinyeh
The car/motorbike/ _____ moped won't start	Машина/мотоцикл/мопед не заводится
	Mushina/muttertsykl/muppyet nyeh zuvvorditsa
Could you call out a _____ mechanic for me, please?	Вызовите скорую техническую помощь, пожалуйста
	Vyzuvveetye skorooyu tyekhneechiskooyu pormushch, puzharlooysta
Could you call a garage_____ for me, please?	Позвоните в гараж, пожалуйста
	Puzvunneetyeh vgurrarsh, puzharlooysta
Could you give me _____ a lift to...?	Вы меня не подвезёте до...?
	Vy minya nyeh pudvizyotyeh duh...?
– a garage/into town?_____	Вы меня не подвезёте до гаража/города?
	Vy minya nyeh pudvizyotyeh duh gur-ruzhar/gorudda?
– a phone booth?_____	Вы меня не подвезёте до телефонной будки?
	Vy minya nyeh pudvizyotyeh duh tyeli-fornoy bootki?
– an emergency phone? ___	Вы меня не подвезёте до аварийного телефона?
	Vy minya nyeh pudvizyotyeh duh uvvurreenuvva tyeliforna?
Can we take my _____ bicycle/moped?	Можно взять велосипед (мотоцикл) с собой?
	Morzhna vzyart vilosipyet (muttatsikl) s suboy?
Could you tow me to _____ a garage?	Вы можете отбуксировать меня до гаража?
	Vy morzhityeh utbookseeruvat minya duh gurruzhar?
There's probably _____ something wrong with...(See page 53)	Скорее всего, что-то с ...
	Skurryayeh fsivor, shtor-to s ...

The parts of a car
(the diagram shows the numbered parts)

	English	Russian	Transliteration
1	battery	аккумулятор	akkoomoolyartur
2	rear light	задняя фара	zardnyaya fara
3	rear-view mirror	зеркало заднего обзора	zyairkulla zardnyivo ubzora
	reversing light	фара для езды задним ходом	fara dlya yizdy zardnim khordum
4	aerial	антенна	untaynna
	car radio	автомобильный радиоприёмник	ufftummubeelny radiopreeyomnik
5	petrol tank	бензобак	binzobark
6	sparking plugs	свечи зажигания	svyaychi zuzhigarniya
	fuel filter/pump	топливный фильтр/насос	torplivny feeltr/nussors
7	wing mirror	наружное зеркало	nuroozhnoyeh zyairkulla
8	bumper	бампер	barmpyer
	carburettor	карбюратор	karbyurartor
	crankcase	масляный картер	marslyuny kartyer
	cylinder	цилиндр	tsyleendr
	ignition	контакты	kuntarkty
	warning light	контрольная лампочка	kuntrorlnaya larmpuchka
	dynamo	динамо	deenarmo
	accelerator	педаль акселератора	pidarl ukselirartora
	handbrake	ручной тормоз	roochnoy tormus
	valve	клапан	klarpun
9	silencer	глушитель	gloosheetyel
10	boot	багажник	buggarzhnik
11	headlight	фара	fara
	crank shaft	коленчатый вал	kullyenchutty varl
12	air filter	воздушный фильтр	vuzdooshny feeltr
	fog lamp	задняя противотуманная фара	zardnyaya pruteevotoomarnnaya fara
13	engine block	моторный блок	muttorny blork
	camshaft	распределительный вал	ruspridyileetyelny varl
	oil filter/pump	масляный фильтр/насос	marslyany feeltr/nussorss
	dipstick	щуп для замера уровня масла	shchoop dlya zummyaira ooruvnya marsla
	pedal	педаль	pidarl
14	door	дверь	dvyer
15	radiator	радиатор	ruddiartor
16	brake disc	тормозной диск	turmuznoy deesk
	spare wheel	запасное колесо	zuppussnor-yeh kullissor
17	indicator	указатель поворота	ookuzzartyel puvvurorta
18	windscreen wiper	дворник	dvornik
19	shock absorbers	амортизаторы	ummurtizartury
	sunroof	раздвижная крыша	ruzzdvizhnahya krysha
	spoiler	спойлер	spoylyer
	starter motor	стартовый двигатель	startuvvy dveeguttyel

On the road | **5**

20	steering column	картер рулевого управления	*karter roolyevorva oopruvlyayniya*
21	exhaust pipe	выхлоп	*vykhlup*
22	seat belt	ремень безопасности	*rimyen byezupparsnusti*
	fan	вентилятор	*ventilyartor*
23	distributor cables	провода свечи зажигания	*pruvuddar svichee zuzhygarniya*
24	gear lever	рычаг переключения передач	*rychark pireeklyoochayniya pireedarch*
25	windscreen water pump	ветровое стекло	*vitruvvoryeh styiklor*
		водяной насос	*vuddyunnoy nussorss*
26	wheel	колесо	*kullissor*
27	hubcap	колпак колеса	*kulpark kullissar*
	piston	поршень	*porshin*

Can you fix it?	Вы можете это починить?
	Vy morzhityeh eto puchineet?
Could you fix my tyre?	Вы можете заклеить шину?
	Vy morzhityeh zukklayit shinoo?
Could you change this wheel?	Вы можете поменять колесо?
	Vy morzhityeh pumminyart kullissor?
Can you fix it so it'll get me to...?	Вы можете это так починить, чтобы я доехал(а) до ...?
	Vy morzhityeh eto tukk puchineet, shtorby ya duhyekhal(a) dor ...?
Which garage can help me?	В каком гараже мне могут помочь?
	Fkukkorm gurruzheh mnyeh morgoot pumorch?
When will my car/bicycle be ready?	Когда моя машина будет готова?/ огда мой велосипед будет готов?
	Kugdar muyah mushina boodyet guttorva?/Kugdar moy vilusipyet boodyet guttorff?
Can I wait for it here?	Вы сделаете это при мне?
	Vy zdyelayetyeh eta pree mnyeh?
How much will it cost?	Сколько это будет стоить?
	Skorlka eta boodyet stor-eet?
Could you itemise the bill?	Вы можете составить подробный счёт?
	Vy morzhityeh sustarveet puddrorbny shchot?
Can I have a receipt for the insurance?	Можно квитанцию для страховки?
	Morzhna kveetarntseeyu dlyah strakhorfki?

5 .8 The bicycle/moped

See the diagram on page 57.

● **Cycle paths** are rare in Russia and there is generally very little special provision on the roads for cycles/mopeds

У меня нет запчастей для вашей машины/вашего велосипеда	I don't have parts for your car/bicycle
Я должен забрать запчасти в другом месте	I have to get the parts from somewhere else
я должен заказать запчасти	I have to order the parts
Это займёт полдня	That'll take half a day
Это займёт день	That'll take a day
Это займёт несколько дней	That'll take several days
Это займёт неделю	That'll take a week
Ваша машина окончательно сломана	Your car is a write-off
Ничего нельзя сделать	It can't be mended
Машина/мотоцикл/мопед /велосипед будет готов(а) в...часов	The car/motor bike/moped/bicycle will be ready at...o'clock

I'd like to rent a... ___	Я бы хотел(а) взять напрокат ...
	Ya by khuttyayl(a) vzyart nupprukkart
Do I need a (special) ___ licence for that?	Для этого нужны специальные права?
	Dlyah etuvva noozhny spetseearlny-yeh pruvvar?
I'd like to rent the...for... ___	Я хочу взять напрокат ... на ...
	Ya khuchoo vzyart nuprukkart ... nah ...
– one day ___	Я хочу взять напрокат ... на один день
	Ya khuchoo vzyart nuprukkart ... nah uddeen dyen
– two days ___	Я хочу взять напрокат ... на два дня
	Ya khuchoo vzyart nuprukkart ... nah dvah dnyah
How much is that per ___ day/week?	Сколько это стоит в день/в неделю?
	Skorlka eto stor-yit v dyen/v nidyaylyu?
How much is the ___ deposit?	Сколько составляет залог?
	Skorlka sustuvlyahyet zullork?
Could I have a receipt ___ for the deposit?	Можно квитанцию об уплате залога?
	Morzhna kveetarntseeyou ub ooplartyeh zullorga?
How much is the ___ surcharge per kilometre?	Какова доплата за километр?
	Kukkuvvar dupplarta za keelomyetr?
Does that include ___ petrol?	Это включая бензин?
	Eto fklyuchahya benzeen?
Does that include ___ insurance?	Это включая страховку?
	Eto fklyuchahya strukhorfkoo?
What time can I pick ___ the...up tomorrow?	Во сколько я могу забрать ... завтра?
	Vuh skorlka ya muggoo zubbrart ... zarftra?
When does the...have ___ to be back?	Когда мне вернуть ... ?
	Kugdar mnyeh virnoot ...?
Where's the petrol tank? ___	Где бак?
	Gdyeh bark?
What sort of fuel does ___ it take?	Какое заливать горючее?
	Kukkoryeh zulleevart gurryoochiyeh?

5 .10 Hitchhiking

● **Hitchhiking** as such should be avoided at all costs and outside the main cities it is in principle not permitted. In major cities use officially marked taxis and do not share them with strangers. Short-distance lifts may be possible in the provinces, but often the drivers regard their cars as unofficial taxis and expect payment, in which case agree the price in advance.

Where are you heading? ___	Куда вы едете?
	Koodar vy yaydyetyeh?
Can I come along? ___	Вы меня не подвезёте?
	Vy minya nyeh puddvizyotyeh?
I'm trying to get to... ___	Мне нужно в...
	Mnyeh noozhna v...
How much will you ___ charge (about)?	Сколько стоит (приблизительно)?
	Skorlka stor-eet (preebleezeetyilna)?

On the road

The parts of a bicycle
(the diagram shows the numbered parts)

No.	English	Russian	Transliteration
1	rear lamp	задний фонарь	*zardnee funnar*
2	rear wheel	заднее колесо	*zardnyeyeh kullissor*
3	(luggage) carrier	багажник	*buggarzhnik*
4	bicycle fork	распределительная головка	*russpridyeleetyelnaya gullorfka*
5	bell	звонок	*zvunnork*
	inner tube	камера шины	*karmera shiny*
	tyre	покрышка шины	*pukkryshka shiny*
6	crank	кривошип	*kreevoship*
7	gear change	цепная передача	*tsipnahya pirreedarcha*
	wire	проволочка	*prorvulluchka*
	dynamo	динамо	*deenahma*
	frame	рама	*rarma*
8	dress guard	сетка	*syetka*
9	chain	цепь	*tsep*
	chain guard	кожух	*kuzhookh*
	chain lock	велосипедный замок	*vilosipyedny zummork*
	milometer	дистанционный спидометр	*distuntsiorny speedormetr*
	child's seat	детское седло	*dyetskoyeh sidlor*
10	headlamp	передний фонарь	*piryaydnee funnar*
	bulb	лампочка	*larmpuchka*
11	pedal	педаль	*pidarl*
12	pump	насос	*nussorss*
13	reflector	рефлектор	*riflyektur*
14	break pad	тормозная колодка	*turmuznahya kullortka*
15	brake cable	тормозной трос	*turmuznoy trorss*
16	ring lock	кольцевой замок	*kultsivoy zummork*
17	carrier straps	резинки	*rizeenki*
	tachometer	спидометр	*speedormetr*
18	spoke	спица	*speetsa*
19	mudguard	крыло	*krylor*
20	handlebar	руль	*rool*
21	chain wheel	зубчатое колесо	*zoopchartoye kullissor*
	toe clip	опора для пальцев ног	*uppora dlya parltsiv nork*
22	crank axle	педальная ось	*pidarlnaya orss*
	drum brake	барабанный тормоз	*burrubbarny tormuss*
23	rim	обод колеса	*orbut kullissar*
24	valve	вентиль	*vyentil*
	valve tube	вентильный шланг	*vyentilny shlank*
25	gear cable	передаточный трос	*pirreedartuchny trorss*
26	fork	вилка переднего колеса	*veelka piryaydnyiva kullissar*
27	front wheel	переднее колесо	*piryaydnyeyeh kullissor*
28	seat	седло	*idlor*

On the road 5

Could you drop me off...?	Вы можете меня высадить в...?
	Vy morzhityeh minya vysuddeet v...?
– here?	Вы можете меня высадить здесь?
	Vy morzhityeh minya vysuddeet zdyess?
– in the centre	Вы можете меня высадить в центре?
	Vy morzhityeh minya vysuddeet v tsentryeh?
Could you stop here please?	Остановитесь здесь, пожалуйста
	Ustunnuveetyes zdyess, puzharlooysta
I'd like to get out here	Я хочу здесь выйти
	Ya khuchoo zdyess vyti
Thanks for the lift	Спасибо, что подвезли
	Spasseebo, shtor puddvizlee

6

Public transport

6 Public transport

6.1 In general

● **Most tourists** go to Russia with an organised party. People who wish to depart from their programme to make, for example, a journey by train, aeroplane or boat, should consult their tour organisers. Payment for longer journeys will probably be in a foreign currency. It is not known whether aircraft maintenance procedures for domestic flights are always properly observed.

Announcements

Поезд на...,время отправления _____ ...,задерживается на...минут...	The train to...at...has been delayed by...minutes
На путь...прибывает поезд _____ на.../из...	The train now arriving at platform...is the train to .../from...
На пути...продолжается _____ посадка на поезд на...	The train to...is still waiting at platform...
Поезд на...отбывает _____ сегодня с...пути	The train to...will leave from platform...
Мы приближаемся к станции..._____	We're now approaching...

Where does this train _____ go to?	Куда идёт этот поезд?
	Koodar eedyot etut por-yest?
Does this boat go to...? ____	Этот теплоход идёт в...?
	Etut tyiplukhort eedyot v...?
Can I take this bus to...? ___	Могу я на этом автобусе доехать до...?
	Muggoo ya na etum aftorboosye du-yekhat doh...?
Does this train stop at...? __	Этот поезд останавливается в...?
	Etut por-yest ustunarvleevahyetsa v...?
Is this seat taken/free/ _____ reserved?	Это место занято/свободно/заказано?
	Eta myesta zarnyutta/svubbordna/zukkarzunna?
I've booked... _____	Я заказывал(а)...
	Ya zukkarzyval(a)...
Could you tell me _____ where I have to get off for...?	Вы не подскажете, где мне выйти для...?
	Vy nyeh puddskarzhityeh, gdyeh mnyeh vyti dlya...?
Could you let me _____ know when we get to...?	Вы предупредите меня, когда мы будем у...?
	Vy pridooprideetyeh minya, kugdah my boodyem oo...?
Could you stop at the _____ next stop, please?	Остановитесь, пожалуйста, на следующей остановке
	Ustunnuvveetyes, puzharlooysta, nah slaydooyushchiy ustunnorfkyeh
Where are we now? _____	Где мы?
	Gdyeh my?
Do I have to get off here? __	Мне здесь выходить?
	Mnyeh zdyess vykhuddeet?

Ticket types

Первый класс или второй класс? _____	First or second class?
В один конец или туда и обратно?_____	Single or return?
Место для курящих или нет? _____	Smoking or non-smoking?
У окна или у прохода? _____	Window or aisle?
Спереди или сзади? _____	Front or back?
Сидячее или спальное место? _____	Seat or couchette?
Наверху, посередине или внизу? _____	Top, middle or bottom?
Туристский класс или _____ бизнес-класс?	Tourist class or business class?
Каюта или сидячее место? _____	Cabin or seat?
Одноместная или двухместная? _____	Single or double?
Сколько вас? _____	How many are travelling?

Have we already _____ passed...?	Мы уже проехали...?
	My oozheh pruyekhali...?
How long have I been _____ asleep?	Сколько я проспал (проспала)?
	Skorlka ya prusparl (pruspullah)?
How long does... _____ stop here?	Сколько времени...простоит здесь?
	Skorlka vraymini...prustuh-eet zdyess?
Can I come back on the____ same ticket?	Можно по этому билету проехать обратно?
	Morzhno po etummoo beelyetoo pruhyekhat ubbrartno?
Can I change on this_____ ticket?	Можно сделать пересадку с этим билетом?
	Morzhno zdyelat pireesartkoo seteem beelyetum?
How long is this ticket _____ valid for?	Сколько времени действителен этот билет?
	Skorlka vraymini dyaystveetyelyen etut beelyet?

Destination

Куда вы едете? _____	Where are you travelling?
Когда вы отъезжаете? _____	When are you leaving?
Ваш...отправляется в..._____	Your...leaves at...
Вам нужно сделать пересадку_____	You have to change trains
Вам нужно выйти в..._____	You have to get off at...
Вам нужно проехать через..._____	You have to travel via...
Поездка туда в... _____	The outward journey is on...
Поездка обратно в... _____	The return journey is on...
Вы должны быть на борту _____ не позже...	You have to be on board by...

Public transport

Inside the vehicle

Ваш билет, пожалуйста	Your ticket, please
Ваш заказ, пожалуйста	Your reservation, please
Ваш паспорт, пожалуйста	Your passport, please
Вы занимаете не то место	You're in the wrong seat
Вы сидите в другом...	You're in the wrong...
Это место зарезервировано /забронировано	This seat is reserved
Вам нужно доплатить	You'll have to pay a supplement
...задерживается на...минут	The...has been delayed by...minutes

6.3 Tickets

Where can I...?	Где можно...?
	Gdyeh morzhno...?
– buy a ticket?	Где можно купить билет?
	Gdyeh morzhno koopeet beelyet?
– make a reservation?	Где можно заказать место?
	Gdyeh morzhno zukkuzzart myesta?
– book a flight?	Где можно купить билет на самолёт?
	Gdyeh morzhno koopeet beelyet nah summalyot?
Could I have a...to..., please?	Можно мне...в...?
	Morzhna mnyeh...v...?
– a single	Можно мне билет в один конец в ...?
	Morzhna mnyeh beelyet v uddeen kun-nyets v...?
– a return	Можно мне билет туда и обратно?
	Morzhna mnyeh beelyet toodar ee ubbrartno?
first class	первый класс
	pyairvy klarss
second class	второй класс
	fturroy klarss
tourist class	туристский класс
	tooreestski klarss
business class	бизнес-класс
	beezniss-klarss
I'd like to book a seat/couchette/cabin	Я хочу заказать сидячее место/спальное место/каюту
	Ya khuchoo zukkuzzart seedyahcheeyeh myesta/sparlnoye myesta/kayootoo
I'd like to book a berth in the sleeping car	Я хочу заказать место в спальном вагоне
	Ya khuchoo zukkuzzart myesta fsparlnum vuggornyeh
top/middle/bottom	наверху/посередине/внизу
	nuvvirkhoo/pussireedeeenyeh/vneezoo
smoking/no smoking	для курящих/некурящих
	dlya kooryahshchikh/nyehkooryahshchikh
by the window	у окна
	oo ukknar

62

single/double _____	одноместный/двухместный
	*uddnam**yest**ny/dvookhm**yest**ny*
at the front/back_____	спереди/сзади
	*s**pay**ridee/s-**zar**di*
There are...of us_____	Нас...человек
	*Narss...chilov**yek***
a car _____	машина
	mushina
a caravan _____	автоприцеп/караван/фургон
	*affta**preetsep**/kurruvv**arn**/foor**gorn***
...bicycles_____	...велосипедов
	*...vilussip**ye**duff*
Do you also have...? _____	У вас есть также...?
	*Oo vuss yest tar**kzheh**...?*
– season tickets? _____	У вас есть также билет для многократного использования?
	*Oo vuss yest tar**kzheh** beel**yet** dlya mnorgak**rart**nuvva eespor**lzuvvarniya**?*
– weekly tickets? _____	У вас есть также абонемент на неделю?
	*Oo vuss yest tar**kzheh** abunnim**yent** nah nid**yay**lyu?*
– monthly tickets? _____	У вас есть также абонемент на месяц?
	*Oo vuss yest tar**kzheh** abunnim**yent** nah m**yay**syets?*

6 .4 Information

Where's...? _____	Где...?
	*G**dyeh**...?*
Where's the information ___ desk?	Где информационная служба?
	*G**dyeh** eenformatsee**or**naya s**l**oozhba?*
Where's the indicator _____ board?	Где табло прибытия/отправления?
	*G**dyeh** tub**blor** pree**by**teeya/uttpruvvl**yay**niya?*
Where's the...desk? _____	Где стол...?
	*G**dyeh** storl...?*
Do you have a city map_____ with the bus/the underground routes on it?	У вас есть план города с указанием автобусов/метро?
	*Oo vuss yest plarn g**orudda** sookuz**arn**iyem aft**orboossoff**/mitror?*
Do you have a _____ timetable?	У вас есть расписание?
	*Oo vuss yest russpees**arneeya**?*
I'd like to confirm/_____ cancel/change my booking for/trip to...	Я хочу подтвердить/аннулировать/ переменить заказ билета в...
	*Ya khuch**oo** puddtveerd**eet**/an**oo**leeruvat/ peerimin**eet** zuk**karss** beel**yeta** v...*
Will I get my money _____ back?	Я могу получить деньги обратно?
	*Ya mug**goo** pulloo**cheet** d**yeng**i ubb**rartna**?*
I want to go to... _____ How do I get there? (What's the quickest way there?)	Мне нужно в...как мне (быстрее) туда доехать?
	*Mnyeh nooz**hna** v...Kukk mnyeh (byst**rayeh**) toodar duh-**yekhat**?*
How much is a _____ single/return to...?	Сколько стоит билет в один конец в...?/ Сколько стоит билет туда и обратно в...?
	*Sk**orl**ka stor-eet beel**yet** vudd**een** kunn**yets** v...?/ Sk**orl**ka stor-eet beel**yet** toodar ee ubb**rartna** v...?*

Do I have to pay a _____ supplement?	Мне нужно доплатить? *Mnyeh noozhnah dupplutteet?*
Can I interrupt my _____ journey with this ticket?	Могу я прервать путешествия с этим билетом? *Muggoo ya prairvat pootyeshestviya setim beelyetum?*
How much luggage _____ am I allowed?	Сколько можно взять багажа с собой? *Skorlka morzhna vzyart buggazhar s-sub-boy?*
Does this...travel direct? ___	Идёт...прямо туда? *Eedyot...pryarma toodar?*
Do I have to change? _____ Where?	Мне нужно пересаживаться? Где? *Mnyeh noozhna pireesarzhivartsa? Gdyeh?*
Will there be any _____ stopovers?	Самолёт делает промежуточные посадки? *Summullyot dyelayet prummizhootuchny-yeh pusatki?*
Does the boat call in at ____ any ports on the way?	Пароход заходит по дороге в гавани? *Purrukhort zukhordit puh durrorgye v garvani?*
Does the train/ _____ bus stop at...?	Поезд/автобус останавливается в...? *Por-yist/aftorbus ustunarvlivahyetsya v...?*
Where should I get off? ____	Где мне выходить? *Gdyeh mnyeh vykhuddeet?*
Is there a connection _____ to...?	Существует связь в...? *Sooshchistvooyet svyaz v...?*
How long do I have to ____ wait?	Сколько мне ждать? *Skorlka mnyeh zhdart?*
When does...leave? _____	Когда отходит...? *Kugdar utkhordit...?*
What time does the _____ first/next/last...leave?	Во сколько идёт первый/следующий/последний...? *Va skorlka eedyot pyairvy/slyay-dooyushchi/pusslyaydni...?*
How long does...take? ____	Сколько времени находится...в пути? *Skorlka vraymini nukhorditsa...fpootee?*
What time does...arrive ____ in...?	Во сколько приходит...в...? *Va skorlka preekhordit...v...?*
Where does the...to... _____ leave from?	Откуда отходит...в...? *Utkoodah uttkhordit...v...?*
Is this...to...? _____	Этот...идёт в...? *Etut...eedyot v...?*

6.5 Aeroplanes

● **On arrival** at a Russian airport, you will find the following signs:

прилёт arrivals отлёт/вылет departures	международный international	внутренние полёты domestic flights

свободно	стоянка такси	занято
for hire	**taxi rank**	**booked**

Taxi! _____	такси!
	Tuksee!
Could you get me a taxi, ___ please?	Вы можете заказать для меня такси?
	Vy morzhitye zukkuzzart dlya minya tuksee?
Where can I find a taxi____ around here?	Где здесь можно поймать такси?
	Gdyeh zdyess morzhna puymart tuksee?
Could you take me to..., ___ please?	Отвезите меня, пожалуйста, в...
	Utvizeetye minya, puzharlooysta, v...
– this address _____	Отвезите меня, пожалуйста, по этому адресу
	Utvizeetye minya, puzharlooysta, po etum-moo ardrissoo
– the...hotel _____	Отвезите меня, пожалуйста, в гостиницу
	Utvizeetye minya, puzharlooysta, v gusteenitsoo
– the town/city centre_____	Отвезите меня, пожалуйста, в центр
	Utvizeetye minya, puzharlooysta, v tsentr
– the station _____	Отвезите меня, пожалуйста, на вокзал
	Utvizeetye minya, puzharlooysta, nah vukkzarl
– the airport _____	Отвезите меня, пожалуйста, в аэропорт
	Utvizeetye minya, puzharlooysta, vairoport
How much is the _____ trip to...?	Сколько стоит поездка в...?
	Skorlka stor-eet pu-yestka v...?
How far is it to...? _____	Как далеко до...?
	Kukk dullikor doh...?
Could you turn on the ____ meter, please?	Включите, пожалуйста, счётчик
	Fklyoocheetye, puzharlooysta, shchotchik
I'm in a hurry _____	Я тороплюсь
	Ya turruplyoos
Could you speed up/ _____ slow down a little?	Вы можете ехать побыстрее/помедленнее?
	Vy morzhitye yekhat pubystray-yeh/pomaydlinyayeh?
Could you take a _____ different route?	Вы можете поехать по другой дороге?
	Vy morzhitye puh-yekhat po droogoy durrorgye?
I'd like to get out here,____ please	Высадите меня здесь
	Vysadeetyeh minya zdyess
You have to go straight ___ on here	Вам нужно здесь ехать прямо
	Varm noozhna zdyess yekhat pryarma
You have to turn left_____ here	Вам нужно здесь повернуть налево
	Varm noozhna zdyess puvirnoot nullyeva
You have to turn right ____ here	Вам нужно здесь повернуть направо
	Varm noozhna zdyess puvirnoot nuprarva
This is it _____	Это здесь
	Eto zdyess
Could you wait a minute___ for me, please?	Вы можете меня минутку подождать?
	Vy morzhitye minya minootkoo pudduzhdart?

6

Public transport

Overnight accommodation

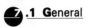 **Overnight accommodation**

7.1 General

● **Going to Russia** on the off-chance and booking hotels when there is still difficult. Most people go as members of a party or as individuals on business and all visa and accommodation arrangements in hotels or campsites are made in advance from Britain.

My name's...I've made _____ a reservation over the phone/by mail	Моя фамилия...я заказывал(а) место (по телефону/письменно) *Muyah fameeliya...ya zukkarzyval(a) myesta (po tyelifornoo/peesminna)*
How much is it per _____ night/week/ month?	Сколько стоит в день/неделю/месяц? *Skorlka stor-eet vdyen/nidyaylyu/myaysits?*
We'll be staying at _____ least...nights/weeks.	Мы пробудем по крайней мере...дней/недель *My prubboodyem po krigh-nyay myairyeh...dnyay/nidyayl*
We don't know yet _____	Мы ещё точно не знаем *My yishchor torchna nyeh znah-yem*

Сколько вы пробудете? _____	How long will you be staying?
Заполните этот бланк, пожалуйста _____	Fill out this form, please
Ваш паспорт, пожалуйста _____	Could I see your passport?
Вам нужно заплатить залог _____	I'll need a deposit
Вам нужно заплатить вперёд _____	You'll have to pay in advance

---

Do you allow pets _____ (cats/dogs)?	Вы допускаете домашних животных (собак/кошек)? *Vy duppooskah-yetyeh dummarshnikh zhivortnykh (subbark/korshik)?*
What time does the _____ gate/door open/close?	Во сколько вы открываете/закрываете ворота/дверь? *Vo skorlka vy utkryvahyetyeh/zukry-vahyetye vurrorta/dvyair?*
Could you get me _____ a taxi, please?	Закажите для меня, пожалуйста, такси *Zukkuzheetyeh dlya minya, puzharlooysta, tuksee*
Is there any mail _____ for me?	Есть почта для меня? *Yest porchta dlya minya?*

.2 **C**amping

See the diagram on page 71.

Where's the manager? _____	Где заведующий?
	Gdyeh zuvvyaydooyushchi?
Are we allowed to _____ camp here?	Мы можем здесь поставить палатку?
	My morzhim zdyess pustarveet pullartkoo?
There are...of us and _____ ...tents	Нас...человек и...палаток
	Narss...chillovyek ee...pullartuk

Вы можете сами выбрать место _____	You can pick your own site
Вам укажут место _____	You'll be allocated a site
Вот номер вашего места _____	This is your site number
Наклейте это на вашу машину, _____ пожалуйста	Stick this on your car, please
Не потеряйте эту карточку, _____ пожалуйста	Please don't lose this card

---

Can we pick our _____ own site?	Мы можем сами выбрать место?
	My morzhim sarmi vybrat myesta?
Do you have a quiet _____ spot for us?	У вас есть тихое местечко для нас?
	Oo vuss yest teekhoyeh mistyechka dlya narss?
Do you have any other ____ sites available?	У вас нет другого свободного места?
	Oo vuss nyet droogorva svubbordnuvva myesta?
It's too windy/sunny/ _____ shady here	Здесь слишком сильный ветер/Здесь слишком солнечно/Здесь слишком много тени
	Zdyess sleeshkum seelny vyaytyer/Zdyess sleeshkum sorlnichna/Zdyess sleeshkum mnorga tyayni
It's too noisy here _____	Здесь слишком шумно
	Zdyess sleeshkum shoomna
The ground's too _____ hard/uneven	Земля слишком твёрдая/неровная
	Zimlyah sleeshkum tvyordaya/nirorvnaya
Do you have a level _____ spot for the camper/caravan/ tents?	У вас есть горизонтальное место для кемпера/каравана/ складного каравана?
	Oo vuss yest gurreezuntarlnoye myesta dlya kyempera/kurruvarna/ skludnorva kurruvarna?
Could we have adjoining __ pitches?	Мы можем стоять рядом?
	My morzhim stuyart ryardum?
Can we park the car _____ next to the tent?	Можно поставить машину около палатки?
	Morzhna pustarvit mashinoo orkulla pullartki?

Overnight accommodation

7

How much is it per _____ person/tent/caravan/car?	Сколько стоит на человека/палатку/караван/машину? *Skorlka stor-it nah chillovyeka/pullartkoo/kurruvvarn/mushi-noo?*
Do you have any _____ bungalows for hire?	Вы сдаёте домики? *Vy zdayotyeh dormeeki?*
Are there any...?_____	Есть ли...? *Yest-lee...?*
–hot showers? _____	Есть ли душ с горячей водой? *Yest-lee doosh zgurryahchi vuddoy?*
– washing machines? _____	Есть ли стиральные машины? *Yest-lee steerarlny-yeh mashiny?*
Is there a...on the site?____	Есть на территории...? *Yest nah territorii...?*
Is there a children's_____ play area on the site?	Есть на территории детская площадка? *Yest nah territorii dyetskaya plushchartka?*
Are there covered _____ cooking facilities on the site?	Есть на территории крытое место для приготовления пищи? *Yest nah territorii krytoyeh myesta dlya preeguttuvlyayniya peeshchi?*
Can I rent a safe here? ____	Можно здесь снять сейф? *Morzhna zdyess snyart syayf?*
Are we allowed to_____ barbecue here?	Здесь можно разжечь барбекю? *Zdyess morzhna ruz-zhaych barbikyoo?*
Are there any power_____ points?	Здесь есть электрические розетки? *Zdyess yest eliktreechiskeeyeh ruzzetki?*
Is there drinking water?____	Здесь есть питьевая вода? *Zdyess yest peetyevahya vuddar?*
When's the rubbish_____ collected?	Когда собирают мусор? *Kugdah subbeerahyut moossur?*
Do you sell gas bottles ____ (butane gas/propane gas)?	Вы продаёте баллоны с газом (бутан/пропан)? *Vy prudda-yotyeh bullorny zgarzum (bootarn/prupparn)?*

.3 Hotel/B&B/apartment/holiday house

Do you have a _____ single/double room available?	У вас есть одноместный/двухместный номер? *Oo vuss yest odnomyestny/dvookhmyestny normer?*
per person/per room _____	с человека/за номер *schilluvvyeka/zah normer*
Does that include _____ breakfast/lunch/dinner?	Это включая завтрак/обед/ ужин? *Eto fklyuchahya zarftruk/ubbyet/oozhin?*
Could we have two_____ adjoining rooms?	Мы можем снять два номера рядом? *My morzhim snyart dvah normera ryardum?*
with/without _____ toilet/bath/shower	с туалетом/ванной/душем; без туалета/ванны/душа *s tooullyetum/varnoy/dooshem; byes tooullyeta/varny/doosha*
(not) facing the street_____	(не) выходящий на улицу *(nyeh) vykhudyashchi nah oolitsu*

Camping equipment
(the diagram shows the numbered parts)

	luggage space	место для багажа	*myesta dlya bugguzhar*
	can opener	открывалка	*utkryvarlka*
	butane gas	баллон с бутаном	*ballorn zbootarnum*
1	pannier	велосипедная сумка	*vilossipyednaya soomka*
2	gas cooker	газовая плитка	*garzuvvaya pleetka*
3	groundsheet	дно палатки	*dnor pullartki*
	mallet	молоток	*mulluttork*
	hammock	гамак	*gamark*
4	jerry can	канистра	*kaneestra*
	campfire	костёр	*kustyor*
5	folding chair	складной стул	*skludnoy stool*
6	insulated picnic box	сумка-холодильник	*soomka-khulludeelnik*
	ice pack	охлаждающий элемент	*okhluzhdahyushchi ellimyent*
	compass	компас	*kormpus*
	wick	фитиль	*feeteel*
	corkscrew	штопор	*shtorpor*
7	airbed	надувной матрац	*nudoovnoy mutrats*
8	airbed plug	затычка от надувного матраца	*zuttychka ut nudoovnorva mutratsa*
	pump	воздушный насос	*vuzdooshny nussorss*
9	awning	навес	*nuvyess*
10	karimat	коврик	*korvreek*
11	pan	кастрюля	*kustryoolya*
12	pan handle	ручка кастрюли	*roochka kustryooli*
	primus stove	примус	*preemoos*
	zip	молния	*morlniya*
13	backpack	рюкзак	*ryookzark*
14	guy rope	тяговый канат	*tyarguvvy kunnart*
	sleeping bag	спальный мешок	*sparlny mishork*
15	storm lantern	фонарь "молния"	*funnar "morlniya"*
	camp bed	раскладушка	*russkluddooshka*
	table	стол	*storl*
16	tent	палатка	*pullartka*
17	tent peg	колышек	*korlyshek*
18	tent pole	палка	*parlka*
	vacuum flask	термос	*tairmus*
19	water bottle	фляжка	*flyashka*
	clothes peg	прищепка	*preeshchepka*
	clothes line	бельевая верёвка	*bilyevahya viryofka*
	windbreak	ветровой щит	*vitruvvoy shcheet*
20	torch	карманный фонарь	*kurrmarny funnar*
	pocket knife	складной нож	*skludnoy norzh*

Overnight accommodation

with/without a view of the sea	с видом на море/без вида на море *sveedum nah moryeh/byez veeda nah moryeh*
Is there...in the hotel?	Есть в гостинице...? *Yest vgusteenitseh...?*
Is there a lift in the hotel?	Есть в гостинице лифт? *Yest vgusteenitseh leeft?*
Could I see the room?	Можно посмотреть номер? *Morzhna pusmutrayt normer?*
I'll take this room	Я сниму этот номер *Ya sneemoo etut normer*
We don't like this one	Этот номер нам не нравится *Etut normer nahm nyeh nrarvitsa*
Do you have a larger/ less expensive room?	У вас есть номер побольше?/У вас есть номер подешевле? *Oo vuss yest normer pubborlsheh?/Oo vuss yest normer puddishevlyeh?*
Could you put in a cot?	Вы можете поставить детсткую кроватку? *Vy morzhityeh pustarvit dyetskooyu kruvartkoo?*

Туалет и душ на том же этаже/ в вашем номере	You can find the toilet and shower on the same floor/en suite
Сюда, пожалуйста	This way, please
Ваша комната на...этаже, номер...	Your room is on the...floor, number...

What time's breakfast?	Во сколько завтрак? *Vuh skorlko zarftruk?*
Where's the dining room?	Где столовая? *Gdyeh stullorvaya?*
Can I have breakfast in my room?	Вы можете принести завтрак в номер? *Vy morzhityeh preenistee zarftruk vnormer?*
Where's the emergency exit/fire escape?	Где запасной выход/пожарная лестница? *Gdyeh zuppusnoy vykhud/puzharnaya lyesnitsa?*
Where can I park my car (safely)?	Где можно надёжно поставить машину? *Gdyeh morzhna nudyozhna pustarveet mushinoo?*
The key to room..., please	Ключ от номера..., пожалуйста *Klyooch ut normera..., puzharlooysta*
Could you put this in the safe, please?	Можно положить это в сейф? *Morzhna pulluzheet eto fsayf?*
Could you wake me at...tomorrow?	Разбудите меня завтра в...часов, пожалуйста *Razboodeetyeh minya zarftra v...chussorf, puzharlooysta*
Could you find a babysitter for me?	Вы можете найти мне няню для ребёнка? *Vy morzhitye nigh-tee mnyeh nyarnyu dlya ribyonka?*

Could I have an extra _____ blanket?	У вас есть ещё одеяло? *Oo vuss yest yishchor uddiyahla?*
What days do the _____ cleaners come in?	По каким дням производится уборка? *Po kukkeem dnyam pruh-eezvorditsa ooborka?*
When are the sheets/ _____ towels/tea towels changed?	Когда меняют постельное бельё/полотенца/кухонные полотенца? *Kugdar minyahyut pustyelnoye bilyor/pul-lutyentsa/kookhunny-yeh pullutyentsa?*

7 .4 Complaints

We can't sleep for _____ the noise	Мы не можем спать из-за шума *My nyeh morzhim spart eez-zah shooma*
Could you turn the _____ radio down, please?	Нельзя ли сделать радио потише? *Nilzyar lee zdyelat rahdio putteesheh?*
We're out of toilet paper ___	Кончилась туалетная бумага *Korncheelas tooullyetnaya boomarga*
There aren't any.../there's ___ not enough...	Нет/недостаточно... *Nyet/nidustartuchna...*
The bed linen's dirty_____	Постельное бельё грязное *Pustyelnoye bilyor gryahznoyeh*
The room hasn't been _____ cleaned.	Комната не убрана *Kormnutta nyeh oobrunna*
The kitchen is not clean____	Кухня не убрана *Kookhnya nyeh oobrunna*
The kitchen utensils are____ dirty	Кухонные принадлежности грязные *Kookhunny-yeh preenudlyezhnusti gryahzny-yeh*
The heater's not_____ working	Отопление не работает *Uttuplayniyeh nyeh rubbortayet*
There's no (hot) _____ water/electricity	Нет (горячей) воды/электричества *Nyet (gurryahchi) vuddy/eliktreechistva*
...is broken_____	...сломан(а) *...slorman(a)*
Could you have that _____ seen to?	Вы можете это починить? *Vy morzhitye eto puchineet?*
Could I have another _____ room/site?	Можно другой номер?/Можно другое место для палатки? *Morzhna droogoy normer? Morzhna droogoryeh myesta dlya pullartki?*
The bed creaks terribly ____	Кровать ужасно скрипит *Kruvvart oozharsna skripeet*
The bed sags _____	Кровать очень прогибается *Kruvvart orchin pruggibahyetsa*
There are insects/ _____ bedbugs in our room	Нас одолевают насекомые/клопы *Nahs uddullivahyut nussikormy-yeh/kluppy*
This place is full_____ of mosquitos	Здесь полно комаров *Zdyess pulnor kummarorff*
– cockroaches_____	Здесь полно тараканов *Zdyess pulnor turrukkarnuff*

Overnight accommodation

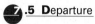

See also 8.2 Settling the bill

I'm leaving tomorrow. _____ Could I settle my bill, please?	Я уезжаю завтра. Рассчитайте меня, пожалуйста *Ya ooyiz-zhahyoo zarftra. Rus-schitigh-tyeh minya, puzharlooysta*
What time should we _____ vacate?	Во сколько мы должны покинуть...? *Va skorlka my dulzhny pukkeenoot...?*
Could I have my deposit/ __ passport back, please?	Можно получить залог/паспорт обратно? *Morzhna pulloocheet zullork/parsspurt ubbrartna?*
We're in a terrible hurry __	Мы очень торопимся *My orchin turrorpimsya*
Could you forward _____ my mail to this address?	Вы можете пересылать мою почту по этому адресу? *Vy morzhityeh peerisylart muyoo porch-too po etummoo ardrisoo?*
Could we leave our_____ luggage here until we leave?	Можно оставить чемоданы здесь до нашего отъезда? *Morzhna ustarveet chimuddarny zdyess duh narshivo utyezda?*
Thanks for your _____ hospitality	Спасибо за гостеприимство *Spasseebo zah gustipree-eemstva*

Overnight accommodation

74

Money matters

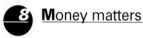

Money matters

● **It is not permitted** to take roubles into or out of Russia. Tourists should take mint-condition foreign currency notes or travellers cheques. Some bank cards can be used at cash machines and in shops in major cities. Cheques are not usually accepted.*Bureaux de change* can be found in hotels, airports, banks and other places. When you change money you must present your passport and declaration form.

8.1 **B**anks

Where can I find a_____ bank/an exchange office around here?	Где здесь поблизости банк/обмен валюты? *Gdyeh zdyess publeezusti barnk/ubmyen vullyooty?*
Where can I cash this_____ traveller's cheque/giro cheque?	Где можно поменять этот чек? *Gdyeh morzhna pumminyart etut chek?*
Can I cash this...here? _____	Можно здесь поменять...? *Morzhna zdyess pumminyart...?*
Can I withdraw money_____ on my credit card here?	Можно получить деньги по кредитной карточке? *Morzhna pulloocheet dyengee po kredeetnoy kartuchkeh?*
What's the minimum/_____ maximum amount?	Каков минимум/максимум? *Kukkorff meeneemum/markseemum?*
Can I take out less_____ than that?	Можно получить меньше? *Morzhna pulloocheet myensheh?*
I've had some money_____ transferred here. Has it arrived yet?	Мне перевели деньги по телеграфу. Они уже пришли? *Mnyeh pirrivillee dyengi po tyelligrarfoo. Unnee oozheh preeshlee?*
These are the details _____ of my bank in the UK	Вот данные моего банка в Великобритании/Англии *Vot darny-yeh muyivvor barnka v Villeekobritarnii/Arnglii*
I'd like to change _____ some money	Я хочу поменять деньги *Ya khuchoo pumminyat dyengi*
– pounds into... _____	Английские фунты на... *Ungleeskiyeh foonty nah...*
– dollars into... _____	Американские доллары на... *Ummerikarnskiyeh dorlary nah...*
What's the exchange _____ rate?	Какой валютный курс? *Kukkoy vullyootny koorss?*
Could you give me some __ small change with it?	Вы можете дать мне часть мелочью? *Vy morzhityeh dart mnyeh charst myeluchyu?*
This is not right _____	Это неправильно *Eto niprarvilna*

Распишитесь здесь _____	**Sign here, please**
Заполните это _____	**Fill this out, please**
Покажите, пожалуйста, паспорт _____	**Could I see your passport, please?**
Покажите, пожалуйста удостоверение личности _____	**Could I see some identification, please?**

8 .2 Settling the bill

Could you put it on_____ my bill?	Запишите на мой счёт, пожалуйста
	Zuppisheetyeh nah moy schot, puzharlooysta
Does this amount _____ include service?	Это включая обслуживание?
	Eto fklyoochahya ubsloozhivarniyeh?
Can I pay by...?_____	Можно заплатить ...?
	Morzhna zupplutteet ...?
Can I pay by credit card?__	Можно заплатить кредитной карточкой?
	Morzhna zupplutteet kredeetnoy kartuchkoy?
Can I pay by traveller's ____ cheque?	Можно заплатить дорожным чеком?
	Morzhna zupplutteet durrorzhnym chekum?
Can I pay with foreign ____ currency?	Можно заплатить иностранной валютой?
	Morzhna zupplutteet eenustrarnoy valyootoy?
You've given me too _____ much/you haven't given me enough change	Вы мне дали слишком много/мало сдачи
	Vy mnyeh darli sleeshkum mnorga/marla zdarchi
Could you check this _____ again, please?	Пересчитайте это, пожалуйста
	Pirrischitigh-tyeh eto, puzharlooysta
Could I have a receipt, ____ please?	Дайте мне, пожалуйста, квитанцию/чек
	Digh-tyeh mnyeh, puzharlooysta, kveetarntsiyoo/chek
I don't have enough _____ money on me	У меня с собой недостаточно денег
	Oo minya s-subboy nidustartuchno dyaynik
We don't accept credit ____ cards/traveller's cheques/foreign currency	Мы не принимаем кредитные карточки/дорожные чеки/ иностранную валюту
	My nyeh prineemahyem kredeetny-yeh kartuchki/durrorzhny-yeh cheki/eenustrarnooyu valyootoo
This is for you _____	Пожалуйста, это вам
	Puzharlooysta, eto varm
Keep the change _____	Оставьте сдачу себе
	Ustarvtye zdarchoo sibyeh

Post and telephone

Post and telephone

9.1 Post

● **Post offices** can also arrange telephone calls and faxes (they have special branches for international calls). Giro cheques are not accepted for payment. Large hotels have agencies that sell stamps, wrap and despatch parcels, and also send faxes. Letterboxes in the street are blue.

почтовые переводы **money orders** посылки **parcels**	марки **stamps**	телеграммы **telegrams**

Where's...?	Где...? *Gdyeh?*
Where's the post office?	Где здесь поблизости почта? *Gdyeh zdyess publeezusti porchta?*
Where's the main post office?	Где главный почтамт? *Gdyeh glarvny puchtarmt?*
Where's the postbox?	Где здесь поблизости почтовый ящик? *Gdyeh zdyess publeezusti puchtorvy yarshchik?*
Which counter should I go to...?	В каком окне можно...? *Fkukkorm uknyeh morzhna...?*
– to change money	В каком окне можно поменять деньги? *Fkukkorm uknyeh morzhna pumminyaht dyengi?*
-for a Telegraph Money Order?	В каком окне можно переслать деньги по телеграфу? *Fkukkorm uknyeh morzhna pireeslart dyengi po tyeligrarfoo?*
Poste restante	До востребования *Doh vustraybuvvarniya*
Is there any mail for me? My name's...	Есть почта для меня? Моя фамилия... *Yest porchta dlya minya? Mu-ya fameeliya...*

Stamps

What's the postage for a...to...?	Какие марки нужны для...в...? *Kukkee-yeh marki noozhny dlya...v...?*
Are there enough stamps on it?	Достаточно марок? *Dustartuchno marukk?*
I'd like... ...rouble stamps	...марок ценой...,пожалуйста *...marukk tsinoy..., puzharlooysta*
I'd like to send this...	Я хочу отправить это... *Ya khuchoo utprarvit eto...*
– express	Я хочу отправить это экспрессом *Ya khuchoo utprarvit eto ekspryessum*
– by air mail	Я хочу отправить это авиапочтой *Ya khuchoo utprarvit eto arviaporchtoy*
– by registered mail	Я хочу отправить это заказным *Ya khuchoo utprarvit eto zukkuznym*

Telegram / fax

I'd like to send a _____ telegram to...	Я хочу отправить телеграмму в... *Ya khuchoo utprarvit tyeligrarmoo v...*
How much is that _____ per word?	Сколько стоит одно слово? *Skorlka stor-eet udnor slorva?*
This is the text I want _____ to send	Вот текст телеграммы *Vort tyekst tyeligrarmy*
Shall I fill out the form _____ myself?	Давайте я заполню бланк сам(а) *Duvvigh-tyeh ya zupporlnyu blarnk sarm (summar)*
Can I photocopy _____ here?	Могу я здесь сделать фотокопию? *Muggoo ya zdyess zdyelat futtakorpiyu?*
Can I send a fax here? ____	Могу я здесь отослать факс? *Muggoo ya zdyess uttuslart farks?*
How much is it _____ per page?	Сколько стоит за страницу? *Skorlka stor-eet za strunneetsoo?*

🌐 .2 Telephone

See also 1.8 Telephone alphabet

● **Telephone kiosks** on the street (автоматы, *ufftummarty*) work with tokens (жетоны, *zhetony*) which can be bought at post offices and elsewhere. Trunk calls and international calls can be made direct from private phones and such calls can also be booked in hotels and special branches of post offices.

Is there a phone box _____ around here?	Здесь есть поблизости телефон-автомат? *Zdyezz **yest** publeezusti tyeliforn-ufftamart?*
Could I use your _____ phone, please?	Можно воспользоваться вашим телефоном? *Morzhna vusporlzuvvartsa varshim tyelifornum?*
Do you have a _____ (city/region)...phone directory?	У вас есть телефонный справочник города .../района...? *Oo vuss **yest** tyeliforny sprarvuchnik gorudda.../righ-orna...?*
Where can I get a _____ phone card?	Дайте мне, пожалуйста,... *Digh-tyeh mnyeh, purzharlooysta,...*
Could you give me...? ____ the number for international directory enquiries	Дайте мне, пожалуйста, номер информации для заграницы *Digh-tyeh mnyeh, purzharlooysta, **no**rmer eenfarmartsii dlya zuggrunneetsy*
– the number of room... ___	Дайте мне, пожалуйста, номер комнаты... *Digh-tyeh mnyeh, purzharlooysta, **no**rmer kormnutty...*
– the code _____	Дайте мне, пожалуйста, код... *Digh-tyeh mnyeh, purzharlooysta, kort...*
– the number of... _____	Дайте мне, пожалуйста, номер... *Digh-tyeh mnyeh, purzharlooysta, **no**rmer...*
Could you check if this ____ number's correct?	Проверьте, пожалуйста, правильность этого номера *Pruvvyairtyeh, puzharlooysta, prarvilnust etuvva normera*

Do I have to go through ___ the switchboard?	Нужно заказывать через телефонистку? *Noozhna zukkarzyvat chayruss tyelifoneestkoo?*
Do I have to dial '0' first? ___	Нужно ли набрать сначала ноль? *Noozhna lee nubbrart snucharla norl?*
Do I have to book _____ my calls?	Нужно ли заказывать разговор? *Noozhna lee zukkarzyvart ruzzguvvor?*
Could you dial this _____ number for me, please?	Наберите мне, пожалуйста, этот номер *Nabirreetyeh mnyeh, puzharlooysta, etut normer*
Could you put me _____ through to.../extension..., please?	Свяжите меня, пожалуйста, с.../номером... *Svyazheetye minya, puzharlooysta, s.../normerum*
What's the charge per _____ minute?	Сколько стоит в минуту? *Skorlka stor-eet vminootoo?*
Have there been any _____ calls for me?	Мне кто-нибудь звонил? *Mnyeh ktor-neeboot zvunneel?*

The conversation

Hello, this is..._____	Здравствуйте, с вами говорит... *Zdrarstvooytyeh, svarmi guvvureet...*
Who is this, please? _____	С кем я говорю? *Skyem ya guvvuryoo?*
Is this...?_____	Я говорю с..? *Ya guvvuryoo s...?*
I'm sorry, I've dialled _____ the wrong number	Извините, я ошибся/ошиблась номером *Eezvinneetyeh, ya ushipsya/ushiblas normerum*
I can't hear you _____	Я вас не слышу *Ya vuss nyeh slyshoo*
I'd like to speak to... _____	Я бы хотел(а) поговорить с... *Ya by khuttyel(a) pugguvvureet s...*
Is there anybody _____ who speaks English?	Кто-нибудь говорит по-английски? *Ktor-niboot guvvureet po-ungleeski?*
Extension..., please_____	Свяжите меня, пожалуйста, с номером... *Svyazheetyeh minya, puzharlooysta, snormerum...*
Could you ask him/her_____ to call me back?	Попросите его/её перезвонить мне, пожалуйста *Pupprusseetyeh yivor/yeyor pirizvunneet mnyeh, puzharlooysta*
My name's... _____ My number's...	Меня зовут.../Мой номер... *Minya zuvvoot.../Moy normer*
Could you tell him/her ____ I called?	Передайте, пожалуйста, что я звонил(а) *Piridigh-tye, puzharlooysta, shtor ya zvunneel(a)*
I'll call back tomorrow ____	Я позвоню ему/ей завтра *Ya puzvunnyoo yimoo/yay zarftra*

Russian	English
Вас к телефону	There's a phone call for you
Наберите сначала ноль	You have to dial '0' first
Секундочку	One moment, please
Ничего не слышно	I can't hear anything
Телефон занят	The line's engaged
Вы подождёте?	Do you want to hold?
Соединяю	Putting you through
Вы ошиблись номером	You've got a wrong number
Его/её в данный момент нет	He's/she's not here right now
Он/она будет на месте...	He'll/she'll be back...
Это автоответчик...	This is the answering machine of...

Shopping

10

Shopping

● **Opening times:** Food shops and markets are open all week, usually from 8.00 a.m. to 9.00 p.m. Other shops usually shut by 8.00 p.m. and have closing days. Foreign currency is not usually accepted, but special foreign currency shops exist. Many shops still have the Soviet system of paying till chits at different counters.

антикварный
магазин
antiques
аптека
pharmacy
'Берёзка'
'Beryozka'
**foreign currency
shop**
булочная/хлеб
bakery
букинистический
магазин
**second-hand book
shop**
вино/винный
магазин
off-licence
гастроном
delicatessen
грампластинки
record shop
дамское бельё
lingerie
игрушки/магазин
игрушек
toys/toyshop
канцтовары
stationery
книги/книжный
магазин
books/bookshop

комиссионный
магазин
second-hand goods
кондитерская
cake shop
кожгалантерея
leather goods
меха
furs
молоко
milk
мясо/мясной магазин
**meat/butcher's
shop**
обувь/магазин обуви
footwear/shoe shop
овощи-фрукты
greengrocer
очки, оптика
opticians
парикмахерская(жен
ская/мужская)
**hairdresser
(ladies'/men's)**
парфюмерия
perfumery
посуда
kitchenware shop
прачечная
laundry
продукты
grocery store

ремонт обуви
shoe repairs
рыба/рыбный
магазин
fish/fish shop
рынок
market
спортивные товары
sports shop
сувениры/магазин
сувениров
**souvenirs/souvenir
shop**
табак/табачный
магазин
tobacco/tobacconist
универмаг
department store
фарфор
china
фототовары
camera shop
хозяйственные
товары
household goods
цветы/цветочный
магазин
flowers/flower shop
электротовары
electrical appliances
ювелирные изделия
jewellers

🔟 .1 **S**hopping conversations

Where can I get...? _____	В каком магазине я могу купить...? *Fkukkorm mugguzeenyeh ya muggoo koopeet...?*
When does this shop _____ open?	Когда работает этот магазин? *Kugdar rubbortayet etut mugguzeen?*
Could you tell me _____ where the...department is?	Покажите мне, пожалуйста, где отдел... *Pukkuzheetyeh mnyeh, puzharlooysta, gdyeh utdyel...*
Could you help me, _____ please? I'm looking for...	Вы мне не поможете? я ищу... *Vy mnyeh nyeh pummorzhityeh? Ya eesh-choo...*

Do you sell English/ _____ American newspapers?	Вы продаёте английские/американские газеты? *Vy pruddayotyeh ungleeskiyeh/ummerikarnskiye guzyayty?*

Вас уже обслуживают? _____ **Are you being served?**

No, I'd like... _____	Нет. я бы хотел(а)... *Nyet. Ya by khuttyel(a)...*
I'm just looking, _____ if that's all right	Я просто хочу посмотреть, если можно *Ya prorsta khuchoo pussmutrayt, yesli morzhna*

Что-нибудь ещё? _____ **Anything else?**

Yes, I'd also like... _____	Да, мне нужно ещё... *Dah, mnyeh noozhna yishchor...*
No, thank you. That's all ___	Нет, спасибо. Это всё *Nyet, spasseeba. Eto fsyo*
Could you show me...? ____	Покажите, пожалуйста,... *Pukkuzheetyeh, puzharlooysta...*
This is not what I'm _____ looking for	Это не то, что я ищу *Eto nyeh tor, shtor ya eeshchoo*
Thank you. I'll keep_____ looking	Спасибо. я поищу в другом месте *Spasseeba. Ya puh-eeshchoo vdroogorm myestyeh*
Do you have _____ something...?	Есть у вас что-нибудь...? *Yest oo vuss shtor-niboot...?*
– less expensive?_____	Есть у вас что-нибудь подешевле? *Yest oo vuss shtor-niboot puddishevlyeh?*
– something smaller?_____	Есть у вас что-нибудь поменьше? *Yest oo vuss shtor-niboot pummensha?*
– something larger? _____	Есть у вас что-нибудь побольше? *Yest oo vuss shtor-niboot pubborlsha?*
I'll take this one _____	Это я возьму *Eto ya vuzmoo*
Does it come with _____ instructions?	Инструкция прилагается? *Eenstrooktsiya preeluggahyetsa?*
It's too expensive _____	Это слишком дорого *Eto sleeshkum dorugga*
I'll give you... _____	Я даю... *Ya dayoo...*
Could you keep this for ____ me? I'll come back for it later	Отложите это, пожалуйста. я скоро вернусь *Utluzheetyeh eto, puzharlooysta. Ya skora virnoos*
Have you got a bag _____ for me, please?	Вы мне не дадите пакет? *Vy mnyeh nyeh duddeetyeh pukkyet?*
Could you giftwrap_____ it, please?	Вы можете это красиво упаковать? *Vy morzhityeh eto krusseeva oopukkuvart?*

Shopping

10

Извините, у нас этого нет _____	I'm sorry, we don't have that
Извините, всё распродано _____	I'm sorry, we're sold out
Извините, это поступит снова..._____	I'm sorry, that won't be in until...
Заплатите в кассе _____	You can pay at the cash desk
Мы не принимаем кредитные _____ карточки	We don't accept credit cards
Мы не принимаем дорожные чеки _____	We don't accept traveller's cheques
Мы не принимаем иностранную_____ валюту	We don't accept foreign currency

🖐 .2 Food

I'd like a hundred_____ grams of..., please	Сто грамм..., пожалуйста *Stor grahm..., puzharlooysta*
– five hundred grams/ _____ half a kilo of...	Полкило..., пожалуйста *Polkeelor..., puzharlooysta*
– a kilo of... _____	Килограмм..., пожалуйста *Keelugrarm..., puzharlooysta*
Could you...it for me, _____ please?	..., пожалуйста *..., puzharlooysta*
Could you slice it/ _____ dice it for me, please?	Порежьте на ломтики/куски, пожалуйста *Purrayzhtyeh nah lormteeki/kooskee, puzharlooysta*
Can I order it?_____	Можно это заказать? *Morzhna eta zukkuzzart?*
I'll pick it up tomorrow/ _____ at...	Я заберу это завтра в...часов *Ya zubbiroo eto zarftra v...chussorf*
Can you eat/drink this? _____	Это можно есть/пить? *Eto morzhna yest/peet?*
What's in it? _____	Из чего это? *Eess chivvor eta?*

🖐 .3 Clothing and shoes

I saw something in the _____ window. Shall I point it out?	Я увидел(а) кое-что на витрине. Давайте покажу *Ya ooveedyel(a) koyeh-shto nah vee-treenyeh. Duvvigh-tyeh pukkuzhoo*
I'd like something to_____ go with this	Я хочу что-нибудь подходящее к этому *Ya khuchoo shtor-niboot pudd-khudyashcheyeh ketummoo*
Do you have shoes _____ to match this?	У вас есть туфли такого же цвета? *Oo vuss yest toofli tukkorva zheh tsvyeta?*
I'm a size...in European _____ terms	Мой размер...по европейской системе *Moy ruzzmyer...puh yevruppyayski seestyaymyeh*
Can I try this on? _____	Можно померить? *Morzhna pummyayreet?*
Where's the fitting room? _____	Где примерочная? *Gdyeh primyairuchnaya?*

Shopping

This is the right size _____	Это мой размер
	Eto moy ruzzmyer
It doesn't suit me_____	Мне не идёт
	Mnyeh nyeh eedyot
Do you have this/ _____ these in...?	У вас это есть в...?
	Oo vuss eto yest v...?
The heel's too high/low ____	Каблук слишком высокий/низкий
	Kublook sleeshkum vysorki/neeski
Is this/are these _____ genuine leather?	Это настоящая кожа?
	Eto nastuyahshchaya korzha?
I'm looking for a... _____ for a...-year-old baby/child	Я ищу...для ребёнка...лет
	Ya eeshchoo...dlya ribyonka...lyet
I'd like it in... _____	Я бы хотел(а)...из
	Ya by khuttyel(a)....eess
– silk _____	Я бы хотел(а)...из шёлка
	Ya by khuttyel(a)... eess sholka
– cotton _____	Я бы хотел(а)...из хлопка
	Ya by khuttyel(a)....eess khlorpka
– wool_____	Я бы хотел(а)...из шерсти
	Ya by khuttyel(a)....eess shairsti
– linen _____	Я бы хотел(а)...из льна
	Ya by khuttyel(a)....eess lnah
What temperature_____ can I wash it at?	При какой температуре можно это стирать?
	Pree kukkoy tyemperatooryeh morzhna eto steerart?
Will it shrink in the _____ wash?	Это садится при стирке?
	Eto suddeetsa pree steerkyeh?

Повесить в намоченном виде	Машинная стирка	Не выжимать в центрифуге
Drip dry	Machine wash	Do not spin dry
Ручная стирка	Химчистка	Не гладить
Hand wash	Dry clean	Do not iron

At the cobbler's

Could you mend _____ these shoes?	Вы можете починить эти туфли?
	Vy morzhityeh puchinneet eti tooflee?
Could you put new _____ soles/heels on these?	Вы можете поставить новые подмётки/каблуки?
	Vy morzhityeh pustarvit norvy-yeh pudmy-otki/kubblookee?
When will they be _____ ready?	Когда они будут готовы?
	Kugdah unnee boodoot guttorvy?
I'd like..., please _____	..., пожалуйста
	..., puzharlooysta
– a tin of shoe polish _____	Банку гуталина, пожалуйста
	Barnkoo gootulleena, puzharlooysta
– a pair of shoelaces_____	Шнурки, пожалуйста
	Shnoorkee, puzharlooysta

I'd like a film for this_____ camera, please	Плёнку для этого фотоаппарата, пожалуйста *Plyonkoo dlya etuvva futta-appurrarta, puzharlooysta*
– a cartridge _____	Кассету, пожалуйста *Kussyetoo, puzharlooysta*
– a one twenty-six _____ cartridge	Кассету "сто двадцать шесть", пожалуйста *Kussyetoo "stor dvartsut shest", puzharlooysta*
– a slide film _____	Плёнку для слайдов, пожалуйста *Plyonkoo dlya sligh-duff, puzharlooysta*
– a videotape _____	Видеокассету, пожалуйста *Veediokussyetoo, puzharlooysta*
colour/black and white____	Цветная/чёрно-белая *Tsvitnahya/chorna-byelaya*
super eight _____	Супер восьмимиллиметровая лента *Soopyer vussmeemeeleemitrovaya lyenta*
12/24/36 exposures _____	Двенадцать/двадцать четыре/тридцать шесть кадров *Dvinartsut/dvartsut chityri/treetsut shest kardruff*
daylight film _____	Плёнка для съёмки при дневном свете *Plyonka dlya s-yomki pree dnivnorm svyetyeh*
film for artificial light _____	Плёнка для съёмки при искусственном свете *Plyonka dlya s-yomki pree eeskoostvinnum svyetyeh*

Problems

Could you load the _____ film for me, please?	Вы можете зарядить фотоаппарат? *Vy morzhityeh zurryuddeet futta-appurrart?*
Could you take the film ____ out for me, please?	Вы можете вынуть плёнку из фотоаппарата? *Vy morzhityeh vynoot plyonkoo eess futta-appurrarta?*
Should I replace_____ the batteries?	Нужно заменить батарейки? *Noozhna zumineet baturrayki?*
Could you have a look_____ at my camera, please? It's not working	Посмотрите, пожалуйста, мой фотоаппарат. Он не работает *Pusmuttreetyeh, puzharlooysta, moy futta-appurrart. Orn nyeh rabortayet*
The...is broken _____	...сломан(а) *...slormun(a)*
The film's jammed _____	Плёнку заело *Plyonkoo zayelo*
The film's broken_____	Плёнка порвалась *Plyonka puhrvullars*
The flash isn't working ____	Вспышка не работает *Fspyshka nyeh rabortayet*

Processing and prints

I'd like to have this film ____ developed/printed, please	Проявите/отпечатайте эту плёнку, пожалуйста *Prayaveetyeh/utpichartightyeh etoo ply-onkoo, puzharlooysta*
I'd like...prints from_____ each negative	...отпечатков с каждого кадра, пожалуйста *...utpichartkoff s karzhduvva kardra, puzharlooysta*
glossy/matt _____	Глянцевый/матовый *Glyantsevy/martuvvy*
6x9_____	Шесть на девять *Shest na dyevit*
I'd like to re-order _____ these photos	Я хочу дополнительно заказать эти фотографии *Ya khuchoo duppulneetyelno zukkuzzart etee futtugrarfii*
I'd like to have this _____ photo enlarged	Мне нужно увеличить эту фотографию *Mnyeh noozhno ooveleechit etoo futtugrarfiyu*
How much is_____ processing?	Сколько стоит проявить? *Skorlka stor-eet pruh-yuvveet?*
– printing _____	Сколько стоит отпечатка? *Skorlka stor-eet utpechartka?*
– it to re-order _____	Сколько стоит дополнительный заказ? *Skorlka stor-eet duppulneetyelny zukkarss?*
– the enlargement_____	Сколько стоит увеличение? *Skorlka stor-eet oovillichayniye?*
When will they_____ be ready?	Когда они будут готовы? *Kugdar unnee boodoot guttorvy?*

🔟 .5 At the hairdresser's

Do I have to make an _____ appointment?	Нужно договориться заранее? *Noozhna dugguvvurreetsa zurrarnye-yeh?*
Can I come in straight ____ away?	Вы можете меня сейчас постричь? *Vy morzhityeh minya say-charss pus-treech?*
How long will I have_____ to wait?	Сколько мне ждать? *Skorlka mnyeh zhdart?*
I'd like a shampoo/ _____ haircut	Я хочу помыть голову/я хочу постричься *Ya khuchoo pummyt gorluvvoo/ya khu-choo pustreechsa*
I'd like a shampoo for ____ oily/dry hair, please	Пожалуйста, шампунь для жирных/сухих волос *Puzharlooysta, shumpoon dlya zheernykh/sookheekh vullorss*
– an anti-dandruff _____ shampoo	Пожалуйста, шампунь против перхоти *Puzharlooysta, shumpoon prorteeff pyairkhutti*
– a shampoo for_____ permed/coloured hair	Пожалуйста, шампунь для химической завивки/крашеных волос *Puzharlooysta, shumpoon dlya kheemeech-eskoy zuvveefki/krarshunykh vullorss*

Shopping

– a colour rinse shampoo __	Пожалуйста, красящий шампунь *Puzharlooysta, krarsyashchi shumpoon*
– a shampoo with _____ conditioner	Пожалуйста, шампунь с ополаскивателем *Puzharlooysta, shumpoon suppullarskivuttyelyem*
Do you have a colour_____ chart, please?	У вас есть гамма цветов? *Oo vuss yest garma tsvitorff?*
I want to keep it the _____ same colour	Такой же цвет, как сейчас *Tukkoy zheh tsvyet, kukk saycharss*
I'd like it darker/lighter_____	Я хочу темнее/светлее *Ya khuchoo timnyay-yeh/svitlyay-yeh*
I'd like/I don't want _____ hairspray	С укрепителем, пожалуйста (без укрепителя, пожалуйста) *Sookrippeetyelyem, puzharlooysta (byes ookkrippeetyelya, puzharlooysta)*
– gel_____	Гель, пожалуйста *Gyel, puzharlooysta*
– lotion _____	Лосьон, пожалуйста *Luss-yon, puzharlooysta*
I'd like a short fringe _____	Короткую чёлку, пожалуйста *Kurrortkooyoo cholkoo, puzharlooysta*
Not too short at the _____ back	Сзади не очень коротко, пожалуйста *S-zardi nyeh orchin korutka, puzharlooysta*
Not too long here _____	Здесь покороче, пожалуйста *Zdyess pukkurorcheh, puzharlooysta*
I'd like/I don't want _____ (many) curls	Завивку, пожалуйста (поменьше кудрей, пожалуйста) *Zuvveefku, puzharlooysta (pummyensheh koodray, puzharlooysta)*
It needs a little/_____ a lot taken off	Отрежьте поменьше/побольше, пожалуйста *Utrayzhtyeh pummyensheh/pubborlsheh, puzharlooysta*
I want a completely _____ different style	Я хочу совсем другую причёску *Ya khuchoo suvsyem droogooyu preechosku*
I'd like it the same... _____	Я хочу причёску как... *Ya khuchoo preechosku kukk...*
– as that lady's _____	Я хочу причёску как у этой женщины *Ya khuchoo preechosku kukk oo etoy zhenshchiny*
– as in this photo_____	Я хочу причёску как на этой фотографии *Ya khuchoo preechosku kukk nah etoy futtugrarfii*
Could you put the _____ drier up/down a bit?	Поставьте, пожалуйста, колпак повыше/пониже *Pustarvtyeh, puzharlooysta, kullpark puvysha/punneezha*
I'd like a facial_____	Маску для лица, пожалуйста *Marskoo dlya leetsah, puzharlooysta*
– a manicure _____	Маникюр, пожалуйста *Munnikyoor, puzharlooysta*
– a massage _____	Массаж, пожалуйста *Massarsh, puzharlooysta*
Could you trim_____ my fringe?	Подстригите мне чёлку, пожалуйста *Puttstreegeetyeh mnyeh cholkoo, puzharlooysta*

– my beard? _____	Подстригите мне бороду, пожалуйста *Puttstreegeetyeh mnyeh boruddoo,* *puzharlooysta*
– my moustache? _____	Подровняйте мне усы, пожалуйста *Puddruvvnyightyeh mnyeh oosy, puzhar-* *looysta*
I'd like a shave, please_____	Побрейте, пожалуйста *Pubbraytyeh, puzharlooysta*
I'd like a wet shave, _____ please	Побрейте меня лезвием, пожалуйста *Pubbraytyeh minya lyayzveeyum, puzhar-* *looysta*

Как вас постричь? _____	How do you want it cut?
Какую бы вы хотели причёску? _____	What style did you have in mind?
Какой сделать цвет? _____	What colour did you want it?
Температура нормальная? _____	Is the temperature all right for you?
Хотите что-нибудь почитать? _____	Would you like something to read?
Хотите что-нибудь пить? _____	Would you like a drink?
Вас всё устраивает? _____	Is this what you had in mind?

At the Tourist Information Centre

At the Tourist Information Centre

11.1 **P**laces of interest

Where's the Tourist Information Centre, please?	Где туристическое бюро? *Gdyeh tooreesteechiskoyeh byooror?*
Do you have a city map?	У вас есть план города? *Oo vuss yest plarn gorrudda?*
Could you give me some information about...?	У вас есть информация о...? *Oo vuss yest eenformartsiya or...?*
How much is that?	Сколько с нас? *Skorlka snarss?*
What are the main places of interest?	Какие самые известные достопримечательности? *Kukkeeyeh sarmy-yeh eezvyestny-yeh dustuppreemichartyelnusti?*
Could you point them out on the map?	Покажите, пожалуйста, на карте *Pukkuzheetyeh, puzharlooysta, nah kartyeh*
What do you recommend?	Что вы нам рекомендуете? *Shtor vy narm rekummendooyetyeh?*
We'll be here for a few hours	Мы пробудем здесь пару часов *My prubboodyum zdyess paroo chussorf*
– a day	Мы пробудем здесь день *My prubboodyum zdyess dyen*
– a week	Мы пробудем здесь неделю *My prubboodyum zdyess nidyaylyu*
We're interested in...	Нас интересует... *Nuss eentyeressooyet...*
Is there a scenic walk around the city?	Мы можем пройтись по городу? *My morzhum pruytees po goruddoo?*
How long does it take?	Сколько это займёт времени? *Skorlka eto zigh-myot vraymini?*
Where does it start/end?	Где начало/конец? *Gdyeh nucharlo/kunnyets?*
Are there any boat cruises here?	Здесь есть теплоходные экскурсии? *Zdyess yest tipplukhordny-yeh ekskoorsii?*
Where can we board?	Где посадка? *Gdyeh pussartka?*
Are there any bus tours?	Есть ли автобусные экскурсии? *Yest-lee ufftorboosny-yeh ekskoorsii?*
Where do we get on?	Где посадка? *Gdyeh pussartka?*
Is there a guide who speaks English?	Есть ли гид, говорящий по-английски? *Yest lee geet, guvvurryashchi pa-ungleeski?*
What trips can we take around the area?	Какие можно сделать вылазки в окрестности? *Kukkeeyeh morzhna zdyelat vylaski vukkryesnusti?*
Are there any excursions?	Есть ли экскурсии? *Yest lee ekskoorsii?*
Where do they go to?	Куда? *Koodar?*

93

We'd like to go to...	Мы хотим в...
	My khutteem v..
How long is the trip?	Сколько длится поездка?
	Skorlka dleetsa puh-yestka?
How long do we stay in...?	Сколько времени мы пробудем в...?
	Skorlka vraymini my prubboodyem v...?
Are there any guided tours?	Будут ли экскурсии?
	Boodoot lee ekskoorsii?
How much free time will we have there?	Сколько у нас будет свободного времени?
	Skorlka oo narss boodyet svubbordnuvva vraymini?
We want to go hiking	Мы хотим в поход
	My khutteem fpukhort
Can we hire a guide?	Можно нанять гида?
	Morzha nunnyat geeda?
What time does... open/close?	Когда открывается/закрывается...?
	Kugdar utkryvahyetsa/zukkryvahyetsa...?
What days is...open/ closed?	По каким дням...открыт/закрыт?
	Puh kakeem dnyam...utkryt/zukkryt?
What's the admission price?	Сколько стоит билет?
	Skorlka stor-eet beelyet?
Is there a group discount?	Есть ли скидка для групп?
	Yest-lee skeetka dlya groop?
Is there a child discount?	Есть ли скидка для детей?
	Yest-lee skeetka dlya dyityay?
Is there a discount for pensioners?	Есть ли скидка для пенсионеров?
	Yest-lee skeetka dlya pinsiunnyairoff?
Can I take (flash) photos	Здесь можно фотографировать (со вспышкой)/снимать?
	Zdyess morzhna futtagruffeerovart (suh fspyshkoy)/sneemart?
Do you have any postcards of...?	У вас есть открытки с...?
	Oo vuss yest utkrytki s...?
Do you have an English...?	У вас есть...на английском?
	Oo vuss yest...nah ungleeskum?
– an English catalogue?	У вас есть каталог на английском?
	Oo vuss yest kuttullork nah ungleeskum?
– an English programme?	У вас есть программа на английском?
	Oo vuss yest prugrarma nah ungleeskum?
– an English brochure?	У вас есть брошюра на английском?
	Oo vuss yest brushoora nah ungleeskum?

11 .2 Going out

● **Tickets for theatres**, opera houses and concert halls can be bought for roubles from their ticket office or from stalls in public places, or for foreign currency through hotels and tourist agencies. Most foreign films are dubbed into Russian.

What's on tonight? _____	Куда сегодня можно пойти? *Koodar sivordnya morzhna puytee?*
We want to go to... _____	Мы хотим в... *My khutteem v...*
Which films are _____ showing?	Какие идут фильмы? *Kukkeeyeh eedoot feelmy?*
What sort of film is that?___	Что это за фильм? *Shtor eto zah feelm?*
Suitable for the whole _____ family	Все возрасты *Fsyeh vorzrusti*
Not suitable for children ___ under twelve/sixteen years	Детям до двенадцати/шестнадцати вход воспрещён *Dyetyum duh dvinartsuti/shistnartsuti fkhort vusprishchon*
original version _____	Недублированный *Nyedoobleeruvvanny*
subtitled _____	С субтитрами *S-soopteetrami*
dubbed _____	Дублированный *Doobleeruvvanny*
Is it a continuous _____ showing?	Без антракта? *Byes untrarkta?*
What's on at...? _____	Что можно посмотреть в...? *Shtor morzhna pussmutrayt v...?*
– the theatre? _____	Что можно посмотреть в театре? *Shtor morzhna pussmutrayt ftyeartreh?*
– the concert hall? _____	Что можно послушать в концертном зале? *Shtor morzhna puslooshat fkuntsairtnum zarlyeh?*
– the opera? _____	Что можно послушать в опере? *Shtor morzhna puslooshat vorpyeryeh?*
Where can I find a good ___ disco around here?	Где здесь хорошая дискотека? *Gdyeh zdyess khurrorshaya deeskutyeka?*
Is it members only? _____	Нужно быть членом? *Noozhna byt chlyenum?*
Where can I find a good ___ nightclub around here?	Где здесь хороший ночной клуб? *Gdyeh zdyess khurrorshiy nuchnoy kloop?*
Is it evening wear only? ___	Вечерняя одежда обязательна? *Vichairnaya uddyezhda ubbyizartyelna?*
Should I/we dress up? _____	Вечерняя одежда желательна? *Vichairnaya uddyezhda zhilartyelna?*
What time does the _____ show start?	Во сколько начинается представление? *Vuh skorlka nuchinahyetsa pridstuvvlyayniye?*

At the Tourist Information Centre

11

When's the next soccer match?	Когда следующий футбольный матч?
	Kudgah slyaydooyushchi footborlny mahch?
Who's playing?	Кто играет?
	Ktor eegrahyet?

11 .3 Booking tickets

Could you book some tickets for us?	Вы можете для нас заказать?
	Vy morzhitye dlya nuss zukkuzzart?
We'd like to book... seats/a table...	Мы хотим...мест/столик
	My khutteem...myest/storlik
– in the stalls	Мы хотим...мест/столик в зале
	My khutteem...myest/storlik vzarlyeh
– on the balcony	Мы хотим...мест/столик на балконе
	My khutteem...myest/storlik nah bulko-rnyeh
– box seats	Мы хотим...мест/столик в ложе
	My khutteem...myest/storlik vlorzheh
– a table at the front	Мы хотим...мест/столик спереди
	My khutteem...myest/storlik spayridi
– in the middle	Мы хотим...мест/столик посередине
	My khutteem...myest/storlik pus-sireedeenyeh
– at the back	Мы хотим...мест/столик сзади
	My khutteem...myest/storlik s-zardi
Could I book...seats for the...o'clock performance?	Можно заказать...мест на представление в...часов?
	Morzhna zukkuzzart...myest nah prid-stuvvlyayniye v...chussorf?
Are there any seats left for tonight?	Есть ещё билеты на вечер?
	Yest yishchor beelyety nah vaychir?
How much is a ticket?	Сколько стоит билет?
	Skorlka stor-eet beelyet?
When can I pick the tickets up?	Когда я могу забрать билеты?
	Kugdar ya muggoo zubbrart beelyety?
I've got a reservation	Я заказывал(а)
	Ya zukkarzyval(a)
My name's...	Моя фамилия...
	Muyah fameeliya

На какое представление вы хотите заказать?	Which performance do you want to book for?
Где вы хотите сидеть?	Where would you like to sit?
Все билеты распроданы	Everything's sold out
Только стоячие места	It's standing room only
Только места на балконе	We've only got balcony seats left
Только места на галёрке	We've only got seats left in the gallery
Только места в зале	We've only got stalls seats left
Только места спереди	We've only got seats left at the front
Только места сзади	We've only got seats left at the back
Сколько мест?	How many seats would you like?
Вы должны забрать билеты до ... часов	You'll have to pick up the tickets before...o'clock
Ваши билеты, пожалуйста	Tickets, please
Вот ваше место	This is your seat

Sports

Sports

12 .1 **S**porting questions

Where can we... _____ around here?	Где мы можем...? *Gdyeh my morzhum...?*
Is there a... _____ around here?	Здесь есть...поблизости? *Zdyess yest...publeezusti?*
Can I hire a...here? _____	Здесь можно взять напрокат...? *Zdyess morzhna vzyaht nupprukkart...?*
Can I take...lessons? _____	Можно брать уроки...? *Morzhna brart oororki...?*
How much is that per_____ hour/per day/a turn?	Сколько это стоит в день/в час/за один раз? *Skorlka eto stor-eet vdyen/fcharss/zah uddeen rahss?*
Do I need a permit _____ for that?	Нужно ли для этого разрешение? *Noozhna lee dlya etuvva ruzrishayniyeh?*
Where can I get _____ the permit?	Где можно получить разрешение? *Gdyeh morzhna puloocheet ruzrishayniye?*

12 .2 **B**y the waterfront

Is it a long way to _____ the sea still?	Ещё далеко до моря? *Yishchor dullikor duh morya?*
Is there a...around here? ___	Здесь есть поблизости также...? *Zdyess yest pubbleezusti tarkzheh...?*
– an outdoor/indoor/_____ public swimming pool	Здесь есть поблизости также бассейн? *Zdyess yest pubbleezusti tarkzheh bussayn?*
– a sandy beach_____	Здесь есть поблизости также песочный пляж? *Zdyess yest pubbleezusti tarkzheh pissorchny plyarsh?*
– a nudist beach_____	Здесь есть поблизости также пляж нудистов? *Zdyess yest pubbleezusti tarkzheh plyarsh noodeestuff?*
– mooring _____	Здесь есть поблизости также пристань для лодок? *Zdyess yest pubbleezusti tarkzheh preestun dlya lorduk?*
Are there any rocks_____ here?	Здесь есть скалы? *Zdyess yest skarly?*
When's high/low tide? _____	Когда прилив/отлив? *Kugdar preeleef/utleef?*
What's the water _____ temperature?	Какова температура воды? *Kukkuvvar tyemperatoora vuddy?*
Is it (very) deep here? _____	Здесь (очень) глубоко? *Zdyess (orchin) gloobukkor?*
Can you stand here?_____	Здесь можно стоять? *Zdyess morzhna stuhyart?*
Is it safe (for children) _____ to swim here?	Здесь безопасно (для детей)? *Zdyess byezupparssno (dlya dyityay)?*

Are there any currents? ____	Есть ли течение?
	Yest-lee tichayniye?
Are there any rapids/ _____ waterfalls in this river?	На этой реке есть стремнины/водопады?
	Nah etoy rikkyeh yest purrorgi/vuddu-pardy?
What does that flag/ _____ buoy mean?	Что означает этот флаг/буй?
	Shtor uznuchahyet etut flahk/booy?
Is there a lifeguard _____ on duty here?	Здесь есть спасательная служба, которая за всем присматривает?
	Zdyess yest spussartyelnaay sloozhba, kuttoraya za fsyem preesmartrivayaet?
Are dogs allowed here? ____	Собакам сюда можно?
	Subbarkum syoodar morzhna?
Is camping on the _____ beach allowed?	Можно поставить палатку на пляже?
	Morzhna pustarvit pullartkoo nah plyarzheh?
Are we allowed to _____ build a fire here?	Можно здесь разжечь костёр?
	Morzhna zdyess ruz-zhaych kustyor?

Место для рыбной ловли	Запрещено купаться	Запрещено повить рыбу
Fishing water	No swimming	No fishing
Опасно!	Запрещено занираться	
Danger	серфингом	
Только с разрешением	No surfing	
Permits only		

🕛 .3 In the snow

Sports

Can I take ski lessons _____ here?	Здесь можно взять уроки по катанию на (горных) лыжах?
	Zdyess morzhna vzyart oororki puh kuttarneeyu nah (gornykh) lyzhakh?
for beginners/advanced ____	Для начинающих/(полу)продвинутых
	Dlya nuchinahyooshchikh/ (pulloo-)prudveenootykh
How large are the _____ groups?	Сколько человек в группах?
	Skorlka chiluvvyek vgroopukh?
What language are _____ the classes in?	На каком языке уроки?
	Nah kukkorm yazykyeh oororki?
Must I give you a _____ passport photo?	Нужна ли фотография для пропуска?
	Noozhnar lee futtagrarfiya dlya prorpuska?
Where can I have a _____ passport photo taken?	Где можно сфотографироваться?
	Gdyeh morzhna sfuttagraffeerovartsa?
Are there any runs for ____ cross-country skiing?	Есть ли поблизости лыжные трассы?
	Yest-lee pubbleezusti lyzhny-yeh trarssy?
Have the cross-country ____ runs been marked?	Лыжные трассы указаны?
	Lyzhny-yeh trarssy ookarzunny?

Sickness

13 **S**ickness

13 .1 **C**all (fetch) the doctor

Could you call/fetch a_____ doctor quickly, please?	Вызовите/найдите скорее врача, пожалуйста
	Vyzzuvveetyeh/nigh-deetyeh skurray-yeh vruchah, puzharlooysta
When does the doctor _____ have surgery?	Когда у врача приём?
	Kugdar oo vruchah preeyom?
When can the doctor _____ come?	Когда врач может прийти?
	Kugdar vrarch morzhit preetee?
I'd like to make an_____ appointment to see the doctor	Назначьте для меня приём у врача, пожалуйста
	Nazznarchtyeh dlya minya preeyom oo vruchah, puzharlooysta
I've got an appointment ___ to see the doctor at...	Мне к врачу к...часам
	Mnyeh kvruchoo k...chussarm
Which doctor/chemist _____ has night/weekend duty?	Какой врач/какая аптека работает ночью/в выходные?
	Kukkoy vrarch/kukkahya uptyeka rubbor- tayet norchyu/v vykhudny-yeh?

13 .2 **P**atient's ailments

I don't feel well _____	Я себя плохо чувствую
	Ya sibya plorkha choostvooyu
I'm dizzy_____	У меня кружится голова
	Oo minya kroozhitsa gulluvar
– ill_____	Я болен (больна)
	Ya borlyen (bulnar)
– sick _____	Меня тошнит
	Minya tushneet
I've got a cold____ _____	Я простудился (простудилась)
	Ya prustoodeelsa (prustoodeelas)
It hurts here _____	У меня здесь болит
	Oo minya zdyess bulleet
I've been throwing up _____	Меня стошнило
	Minya stushneela
I've got... _____	У меня болит...
	Oo minya bulleet...
I'm running a _____ temperature of...degrees.	У меня температура...градусов
	Oo minya tyemperatoora...grardoosuff
I've been stung by_____ a wasp	Меня укусила оса
	Minya ookooseela ussar
I've been stung by an_____ insect	Меня укусило насекомое
	Minya ookooseela nassikormoyeh
I've been bitten by _____ a dog	Меня укусила собака
	Minya ookooseela subbarka
I've been stung by_____ a jellyfish	Меня ужалила медуза
	Minya oozharleela midooza
I've been bitten by _____ a snake	Меня ужалила змея
	Minya oozharleela zmiyah
I've been bitten by _____ an animal	Меня укусил зверь
	Minya ookooseel zvyair

I've cut myself	Я порезался (порезалась)
	Ya puhryezalsya (puhryezalas)
I've burned myself	Я обжёгся (обожглась)
	Ya ubzhoksa (ubuzhglarss)
I've grazed myself	Я ободрал (ободрала)...
	Ya ubbudrarl (ubbudrullar)...
I've had a fall	Я упал(а)
	Ya ooparl(a)
I've sprained my ankle	Я вывихнул(а) щиколотку
	Ya vyvikhnool(a) shchikullortkoo

🖐 .3 The consultation

🤝

На что жалуетесь?	What seems to be the problem?
Как долго вы на это жалуетесь?	How long have you had these complaints?
У вас уже было подобное раньше?	Have you had this trouble before?
Какая у вас температура?	How high is your temperature?
Разденьтесь, пожалуйста	Get undressed, please
Разденьтесь до пояса, пожалуйста	Strip to the waist, please
Вы можете там раздеться	You can undress there
Обнажите левую/правую руку, пожалуйста	Roll up your left/right sleeve, please
Лягте здесь, пожалуйста	Lie down here, please
Больно?	Does this hurt?
Дышите глубоко	Breathe deeply
Откройте рот	Open your mouth

Patient's medical history

I'm a diabetic	У меня диабет
	Oo minya diabyet
I have a heart condition	У меня больное сердце
	Oo minya bullnor-yeh sairtseh
I have asthma	У меня астма
	Oo minya arstma
I'm allergic to...	У меня аллергия на...
	Oo minya ullairgeeya nah...
I'm...months pregnant	Я на...месяце беременности
	Ya nah...myaysyutseh biryayminusti
I'm on a diet	Я на диете
	Ya nah deeyetyeh
I'm on medication/the pill	Я принимаю лекарства/противозачаточные таблетки
	Ya preeneemahyu likarstva/prutee-vazuchartuchny-yeh tublyetki
I've had a heart attack once before	У меня уже был раньше приступ сердца
	Oo minya oozheh byl rarnsheh preestoop sairtsa

I've had a(n)...operation	У меня была операция на...
	Oo minya bylar uppirartsiya nah...
I've been ill recently	Я только что переболел(а)
	Ya torlka shtor pirribullyel(a)
I've got an ulcer	У меня язва желудка
	Oo minya yarzva zhillootka
I've got my period	У меня менструация
	Oo minya menstrooartsiya

У вас есть аллергия на что-нибудь?	Do you have any allergies?
Принимаете лекарства?	Are you on any medication?
Вы на диете?	Are you on a diet?
Вы беременны?	Are you pregnant?
Вам делали прививку от столбняка?	Have you had a tetanus injection?

The diagnosis

Ничего серьёзного	It's nothing serious
Вы сломали...	Your...is broken
Вы ушибли...	You've got a/some bruised...
Вы порвали...	You've got (a) torn...
У вас воспаление	You've got an inflammation
У вас аппендицит	You've got appendicitis
У вас бронхит	You've got bronchitis
У вас венерическая болезнь	You've got a venereal disease
У вас грипп	You've got the 'flu
У вас был сердечный приступ	You've had a heart attack
У вас (вирусная, бактериологическая) инфекция	You've got an infection (viral, bacterial)
У вас воспаление лёгких	You've got pneumonia
У вас язва желудка	You've got a stomach ulcer
Вы растянули мышцу	You've pulled a muscle
У вас инфекция во влагалище	You've got a vaginal infection
У вас пищевое отравление	You've got food poisoning
У вас солнечный удар	You've got sunstroke
У вас аллергия на ...	You're allergic to...
Вы беременны	You're pregnant
Я хочу исследовать вашу кровь/мочу/кал	I'd like to have your blood/urine/stools tested
Необходимо зашить	It needs stitching
Я вас направляю к специалисту/в больницу	I'm referring you to a specialist/sending you to hospital

Sickness

13

Нужно сделать снимки _____ _____	You'll need to have some x-rays taken
Подождите, пожалуйста, _____в приёмнойroom,	Could you wait in the waiting room, please?
Необходима операция_____	You'll need an operation

Is it contagious?_____	Это заразно? *Eto zurrarzna?*
How long do I have to _____ stay...?	Сколько мне придётся пробыть...? *Skorlka mnyeh preedyotsa prubbyt...?*
– in bed _____	Сколько мне придётся пробыть в постели? *Skorlka mnyeh preedyotsa prubbyt fpustyayli?*
– in hospital _____	Сколько мне придётся пробыть в больнице? *Skorlka mnyeh preedyotsa prubbyt vbulneetseh?*
Do I have to go on _____ a special diet?	Мне нужно сесть на диету? *Mnyeh noozhna syest na dee-etoo?*
Am I allowed to travel? ____	Мне можно путешествовать? *Mnyeh morzhna pootyeshestvuvvart?*
Can I make a new _____ appointment?	Можно с вами договориться на следующий раз? *Morzhna svarmi dugguvvurreetsa na slyaydooyushchiy rahss?*
When do I have to_____ come back?	Когда мне снова прийти? *Kugdar mnyeh snorva preetee?*
I'll come back _____ tomorrow	Я приду завтра снова *Ya preedoo zarftra snorva*

Вы должны снова прийти _____ завтра/через ... дней_____	Come back tomorrow/in...days' time.

🕙 .4 Medication and prescriptions

How do I take this _____ medicine?	Как принимать это лекарство? *Kukk preeneemart eto likarstva?*
How many capsules/ _____ drops/injections/ spoonfuls/tablets each time?	Сколько капсул/капель/уколов/ложек/ таблеток за раз? *Skorlka karpsool/karpyel/ookorluff/ lorzhik/tubblyetuk zah rahss?*
How many times a day? ___	Сколько раз в день? *Skorlka rahss vdyen?*
I've forgotten my_____ medication. At home I take...	Я забыл(а) лекарства. Дома я принимаю... *Ya zubbyl(a) likarstva. Dorma ya pree- neemahyu...*
Could you make out a _____ prescription for me?	Выпишите мне рецепт, пожалуйста *Vypishytyeh mnyeh ritsept, puzharlooysta*

я вам прописываю антибиотики/_____ микстуру/успокаивающее средство/ болеутоляющие средства	I'm prescribing antibiotics/a mixture/a tranquillizer/pain killers
Необходим покой _____	Have lots of rest
Вам нельзя выходить на улицу_____	Stay indoors
Вы должны оставаться в постели_____	Stay in bed

в течение...дней for...days	перед едой before meals	только для наружного употребления
завершить лечение to finish the course	принимать to take	not for internal use
каждые...часов every...hours	...раз в сутки... times a day	уколы injections
капли drops	растворить в воде to dissolve in water	целиком проглатывать swallow whole
капсулы capsules	столовые/чайные ложки tablespoons/ teaspoons	эти лекарства влияют на способность управлять машиной this medication impairs your driving
мазать rub on		
мазь ointment	таблетки tablets	

13 .5 At the dentist's

English	Russian
Do you know a good _____ dentist?	Вы не знаете хорошего зубного врача? *Vy nyeh znahyetye khurrorshivo zoobnor-va vruchar?*
Could you make a _____ dentist's appointment for me? It's urgent	Запишите меня на приём к зубному врачу, пожалуйста. Мне нужно срочно. *Zuppishytyeh minya nah preeyom k zoobnormoo vruchoo, puzharlooysta. Mnyeh noozhna srorchna.*
Can I come in today,_____ please?	Мне можно прийти прямо сегодня? *Mnyeh morzhna preetee pryarma sivord-nya?*
I have (terrible)_____ toothache	У меня (ужасно) болит зуб *Oo minya oozharssno bulleet zoop*
Could you prescribe/ _____ give me a painkiller?	Вы можете мне прописать/дать болеутоляющее? *Vy morzhityeh mnyeh pruppeessart/dart borlyeootullyahyooshchiyeh?*
A piece of my tooth _____ has broken off	У меня отломился кусочек зуба *Oo minya ullammeelsya koosorchek zooba*
My filling's come out _____	У меня выпала пломба *Oo minya vypala plormba.*
I've got a broken crown____	У меня сломалась коронка *Oo minya slummarlas kurrornka*
I'd like/I don't want a _____ local anaesthetic	Я хочу/не хочу местный наркоз *Ya khuchoo/nyeh khuchoo myestny narkorss*

Can you do a makeshift_____ repair job?	Вы можете мне временно помочь?
	Vy morzhityeh mnyeh vrayminna pummorch?
I don't want this tooth _____ pulled	Не вырывайте этот зуб
	Nyeh vyryvightyeh etut zoop
My dentures are broken. ___ Can you fix them?	У меня сломался протез. Вы можете его починить?
	Oo minya slummarlsya pruttess. Vy morzhityeh yivvor puchineet?

Какой зуб болит? _____	Which tooth hurts?
У вас нарыв _____	You've got an abscess
Нужно обработать нерв _____	I'll have to do a root canal
Я сделаю местный наркоз_____	I'm giving you a local anaesthetic
Нужно этот зуб запломбировать _____ вырвать/обточить	I'll have to fill/pull out/grind this tooth down
Нужно сверлить _____	I'll have to drill
Откройте рот_____	Open wide, please
Закройте рот _____	Close your mouth, please
Прополощите _____	Rinse, please
Всё ещё болит?_____	Does it hurt still?

14

In trouble

14 In trouble

14 .1 Asking for help

Help! _____ Помогите!
Pummugeetyeh!

Fire! _____ Пожар!
Puzhar!

Police! _____ Милиция!
Meeleetsiya!

Quick! _____ Быстро!
Bystra!

Danger! _____ Опасно!
Upparsna!

Watch out! _____ Осторожно!
Usturrorzhna!

Stop! _____ Стоп!
Storp!

Be careful! _____ Осторожно!
Usturrorzhna!

Don't! _____ Не надо!
Nyeh narda!

Let go! _____ Отпустите!
Utpoosteetyeh!

Stop that thief! _____ Держи вора!
Dyerzhee vora!

Could you help me, _____ Помогите, пожалуйста
please? *Pummuggeetyeh, puzharlooysta*

Where's the police _____ Где отделение милиции?/где запасной
station/emergency выход?/где пожарная лестница?
exit/fire escape? *Gdyeh utdilyayniyeh mileetsii?/gdyeh zup-*
pussnoy vykhud?/gdyeh puzharnaya
lyesnitsa?

Where's the nearest fire _____ Где огнетушитель?
extinguisher? *Gdyeh ugnyetoosheetyel?*

Call the fire brigade! _____ Предупредите пожарную команду!
Predoopriddeetyeh puzharnooyu
kummarndoo!

Call the police! _____ Позвоните в милицию!
Puzvunneetyeh vmileetsiyu!

Call an ambulance! _____ Вызовите скорую помощь!
Vyzuvveetyeh skorooyu pormushch!

Where's the nearest _____ Где телефон?
phone? *Gdyeh tyeliforn?*

Could I use your phone? _____ Можно позвонить по вашему телефону?
Morzhna puzvunneet puh varshimoo
tyelifornoo?

What's the number for _____ Какой телефон вызова милиции?
the police? *Kukkoy tyeliforn vyzuvva mileetsii?*

⑭ .2 Loss

I've lost my purse/_____ wallet	Я потерял(a) кошелёк/бумажник *Ya puttyiryarl(a) kushilyok/boomarzhnik*
I lost my...yesterday _____	Я вчера забыл(a) ... *Ya vchirar zubbyl(a) ...*
I left my...here _____	Я здесь оставил(a) ... *Ya zdyess ustarveel(a) ...*
Did you find my...? _____	Вы не находили ...? *Vy nyeh nukhuddeeli ...?*
It was right here_____	Он стоял/лежал здесь *Orn stuh-yarl/lyizharl zdyess*
It's quite valuable _____	Это очень ценная вещь *Eto orchin tsen-naya vyeshch*
Where's the lost_____ property office?	Где бюро находок? *Gdyeh byooror nukhordukk?*

⑭ .3 Accidents

There's been an accident __	Произошёл несчастный случай *Pruh-eezoshorl nischarstny sloochay*
Someone's fallen into _____ the water	Человек упал в воду *Chiluvvyek ooparl v vordoo*
There's a fire_____	Пожар *Puzhar*
Is anyone hurt? _____	Кто-нибудь ранен? *Ktor-neeboot rarnyun?*
Some people have _____ been/no one's been injured	Есть пострадавшие (нет пострадавших) *Yest pustruddarfsheeyeh (nyet pustruddarfshikh)*
There's someone in _____ the car/train still	Ещё кто-то остался в машине/поезде *Yishchor ktor-to ustarlsya vmushinyeh/por-yizdyeh*
It's not too bad. Don't_____ worry	Ничего страшного. Не беспокойтесь *Nichivvor strarshnuvva. Nyeh byespukkoy-tyes*
Leave everything the _____ way it is, please	Ничего не трогайте *Nichivvor nyeh trorgightyeh*
I want to talk to the_____ police first	Я хочу сначала поговорить с милицией *Ya khuchoo snucharla pugguvvurreet smileetsiyay*
I want to take a _____ photo first	Я хочу сначала сфотографировать *Ya khuchoo snucharla sfuttagruffeerovat*
Here's my name_____ and address	Вот моя фамилия и адрес *Vort muh-yah fameeliya ee ardriss*
Could I have your _____ name and address?	Можно вашу фамилию и адрес? *Morzhna varshoo fameeliyu i ardriss?*
Could I see some_____ identification/your insurance papers?	Можно ваше удостоверение личности?/Можно вашу страховку? *Morzhna varsha oodustuvviryayniyeh leechnusti? Morzhna varshoo strukhofkoo?*
Will you act as a _____ witness?	Вы хотите быть свидетелем? *Vy khutteetyeh byt sveedyaytyelyum?*
I need the details for _____ the insurance	Мне нужны данные для страховки *Mnyeh noozhny darn-ny-yeh dlya strukhofki*

In trouble

14

110

Are you insured? _____	Вы застрахованы?
	Vy zustrukhorvany?
Could you sign here, _____ please?	Распишитесь здесь, пожалуйста
	Rasspishytyes zdyess, puzharlooysta

 .4 Theft

I've been robbed _____	Меня обокрали
	Minya ubbukkrarli
My...has been stolen _____	У меня украли...
	Oo minya ookrarli...
My car's been _____ broken into	Моя машина взломана
	Muy-ya mushina vzlormunna

 .5 Missing person

I've lost my child/ _____ grandmother	Я потерял(а) ребёнка/бабушку
	Ya putyiryarl(a) ribyonka/barbooshku
Could you help me _____ find him/her?	Вы мне поможете искать?
	Vy mnyeh pummorzhityeh eeskart?
Have you seen a _____ small child?	Вы не видели ребёнка?
	Vy nyeh veedyeli ribyonka?
He's/she's...years old _____	Ему/ей...лет
	Yimoo/yay...lyet
He's/she's got _____ short/long/blonde/red/ brown/black/grey/curly/ straight/frizzy hair	У него/неё короткие/длинные/светлые/ рыжие/каштановые/тёмные/седые/кудряв ые/прямые/ вьющиеся волосы
	Oo nyivvor/nyiyor kurrortkiyeh/dleeny-yeh/svyetly-yeh/ryzhiyeh/ kushtarnuvy-yeh/tyomny-yeh/sidy-yeh/koodryarvy-yeh/pryummy-yeh/v-yooshchiyehsya vorlussy
with a ponytail _____	С хвостиком
	Skhvorstikum
with plaits _____	С косичками
	Skusseechkummi
in a bun _____	С пучком
	Spoochkorm
He's/she's got _____ blue/brown/green eyes	Глаза голубые/карие/зелёные
	Gluzzah gullooby-yeh/kariyeh/zilyony-yeh
He's wearing swimming ___ trunks/mountaineering boots	На нём плавки/горные ботинки
	Nah nyom plarfki/gorny-yeh butteenki
with/without glasses/ _____ a bag	В очках/без очков, с сумкой/без сумки
	Vuchkarkh/byez uchkorff, s-soomkoy/byes soomki
tall/short_____	Большой (большая)/маленький (маленькая)
	Bulshoy (bulshaya)/marlinki (marlinkaya)
This is a photo of _____ him/her	Вот его/её фотография
	Vort yivvor/yiyor futtagrarfiya
He/she must be lost _____	Он/она, скорее всего, заблудился (заблудилась)
	Orn/unnar, skurryay-yeh fsivvor, zubbloodeelsya (zubbloodeelas)

In trouble

14

An arrest

Ваши документы на машину, _____ пожалуйста	Your vehicle registration papers, please
Вы превысили скорость _____	You were speeding
Вы нарушили правила стоянки _____	You're not allowed to park here
У вас не работают фары _____	Your lights aren't working
С вас штраф... _____	You are fined...
Вы можете сразу заплатить? _____	Can you pay on the spot?
Вам нужно сразу заплатить _____	You must pay on the spot

I don't speak Russian _____   Я не говорю по-русски
                           *Ya nyeh guvvurr**yoo** puh-roo**ski***

I didn't see the sign _____   Я не видел(а) этого знака
                           *Ya nyeh **vee**dyel(a) **e**tuvva zn**ar**ka*

I don't understand _____
   what it says   Я не понимаю, что там написано
                           *Ya nyeh punni**mah**yu, shtor tarm nup-pee**sunna***

I was only doing... _____
   kilometres an hour   Я ехал(а) всего...километров в час
                           *Ya **ye**khal(a) fsivv**or**...**kee**lummyetruff fcharss*

I'll have my car checked ___   Я отдам проверить машину
                           *Ya ut**d**arm pruvvy**ai**rit mushi**noo***

I was blinded by _____
   oncoming lights   Меня ослепил встречный свет
                           *Min**ya** uslyep**ee**l fstr**ay**chny svyet*

Где это случилось? _____	Where did it happen?
Что вы потеряли? _____	What's missing?
Что украдено? _____	What's been stolen?
Можно ваше удостоверение _____ личности?	Could I see some identification?
Когда это произошло? _____	What time did it happen?
Кто при этом присутствовал? _____	Who was there?
Свидетели есть? _____	Are there any witnesses?
Заполните, пожалуйста _____	Fill this out, please
Подпишите здесь, пожалуйста _____	Sign here, please
Вам нужен переводчик? _____	Do you want an interpreter?

In trouble

14

At the police station

I want to report a _____ collision/a theft/rape	Я хочу сообщить об аварии/о потере/об изнасиловании *Ya khuchoo suh-ubshcheet ub avarii/o puttyairyeh/ub eeznusseeluvarnii*
Could you make out _____ a report, please?	Составьте протокол, пожалуйста *Sustarvtyeh pruttukkorl, puzharlooysta*
Could I have a copy _____ for the insurance?	Можно справку для страховки? *Morzhna sprarfkoo dlya strukhorfki?*
I've lost everything _____	Я всё потерял(а) *Ya fsyo puttyeryarl(a)*
My money has run _____ out and I don't know what to do	У меня кончились деньги, я совершенно растерян(а) *Oo minya korncheelees dyengi, ya suvvir-shenna rastyeryun(a)*
I'd like an interpreter _____	Мне нужен переводчик *Mnyeh noozhun pirivortchik*
I'm innocent _____	Я не виноват(а) *Ya nyeh veenuvvart(a)*
I don't know anything ____ about it	Я ничего не знаю *Ya nichivvor nyeh znahyu*
I want to speak to _____ someone from the British consulate	Я хочу поговорить с кем-нибудь из консульства Великобритании *Ya khuchoo pugguvvurreet skyem-nee-boot eess kornsoolstva Vileekobrittanii*
I need to see someone ____ from the British embassy	Я хочу поговорить с кем-нибудь из посольства Великобритании *Ya khuchoo pugguvvurreet skyem-nee-boot eess pussorlstva Vileekobrittarnii*
I want a lawyer who _____ speaks English	Мне нужен адвокат, который говорит по-английски/по *Mnyeh noozhun udvukkart, kuttory guvvurreet puh-ungleeski/puh*

In trouble

14

15

Word list

Word list English - Russian

● **This word list** is intended to supplement the previous chapters. In a number of cases, words not included in this list can be found elsewhere in the book, for example alongside the diagrams of the car, the bicycle and the camping equipment. Many food words can be found in the Russian-English list in 4.7.
Abbreviations used: n=noun, vb=verb, adj=adjective, advb=adverb.
With adjectives the masculine form is given, sometimes with the feminine in brackets.

A

above	наверху	navirkh**oo**
abroad	заграница	zuggrunn**ee**tsa
accident	несчастный случай	nyehshch**a**rstny sl**oo**chigh
adder	гадюка	gudd**yoo**ka
addition (maths)	сложение	sluzh**ay**niyeh
address	адрес	**a**rdriss
admission	вход	fkh**o**rt
admission price	входная плата	fkhudd**na**hya pl**a**rta
advice	совет	suvv**ye**t
after	после	p**o**rsslyeh
afternoon	днём	dn**yo**m
aftershave	одеколон после бритья	uddikull**orn** p**o**rslyeh br**ee**tyah
again	снова	sn**o**rva
against	против	pr**o**rteef
age	возраст	v**o**rzrust
Aids	СПИД	SP**EE**T
air conditioning	кондиционер	kundeetsiony**a**ir
air mattress	надувной матрац	nudd**oo**vnoy m**u**ttrats
air sickness bag	гигиенический пакет	geegeeyen**ee**cheski pukk**ye**t
aircraft	самолёт	summal**yo**t
airmail (by)	авиапочтой	arviap**o**rchtoy
airport	аэропорт	ah-airupp**o**rt
airport	аэропорт	ah-airop**o**rt
alarm	тревога	triv**o**rga
alarm clock	будильник	bood**ee**lnik
alcohol	алкоголь	alkugg**o**rl
alcoholic drink	спиртной напиток	speertn**oy** nupp**ee**tuk
all the time	постоянно	pustuhy**a**nno
allergic	аллергический	ullyerg**ee**cheski
alone	один (одна)	udd**ee**n (udd**na**r)
always	всегда	fsigd**a**r
ambulance	скорая (помощь)	sk**o**raya (p**o**rmushch)
amount	сумма	s**oo**m-ma
amusement park	парк отдыха (и развлечений)	park **o**rtdykha (ee razvlich**a**ynee)
anaesthetize	обезболить	ubbyuzb**o**rleet
anchovy	анчоус	unch**o**r-oos
and	и	ee
angry	сердитый	syaird**ee**ty
animal	животное	zhivv**o**rtnoyeh
ankle	лодыжка	ludd**y**shka
answer	ответ	utv**ye**t
ant	муравей	mooruvv**a**y

antibiotics	антибиотик	*untibeeortik*
antifreeze	антифриз	*untifreess*
antique	античный	*unteechny*
antiques	антикварная вещь	*untikvarnaya vyeshch*
anus	задний проход	*zardni prukhort*
apartment	квартира	*kvarteera*
aperitif	аперитив	*uppyereeteef*
apologies	извинения	*eezvinyayniya*
apple	яблоко	*yarblukka*
apple juice	яблочный сок	*yarbluchny sork*
apple pie	пирог с яблоками	*peerork syarblukkummi*
apple sauce	яблочный мусс	*yarbluchny mooss*
appointment	приём	*preeyom*
approximately	приблизительно	*preebleezeetyelna*
apricot	абрикос	*ubbreekorss*
April	апрель	*upryel*
archbishop	архиепископ	*arkhiyepeeskup*
architecture	архитектура	*arkhityektoora*
area	окрестность	*ukryesnust*
arm	рука	*rookar*
arrange	договориться	*dugguvvureetsa*
arrive	прийти/приехать	*preetee/preeyekhat*
arrow	стрела	*strillar*
art	искусство	*eeskoostva*
artery	артерия	*artyayreeya*
artichokes	артишоки	*artishorki*
article	товар	*tuvvar*
artificial respiration	искусственное дыхание	*eeskoostven-noyeh dykharniyeh*
arts and crafts	прикладное искусство	*preekludnoryeh eeskoostva*
ashtray	пепельница	*pyaypilneetsa*
ask (for)	просить	*prusseet*
ask (question)	спросить	*sprusseet*
asparagus	спаржа	*sparzha*
aspirin	аспирин	*aspeereen*
assault	попытка к изнасилованию	*puppytka keeznussee luvvarniyu*
at once	сразу	*srarzoo*
at the front	впереди	*fpiridee*
at the latest	не позже	*nyeh porzheh*
aubergine	баклажан	*bukkluzharn*
August	август	*arvgoost*
automatic	автоматический	*ufftummutteecheski*
autumn	осень	*orsin*
avalanche	лавина	*luveena*
awake	проснувшись	*prusnoofshees*
awning	ширма от солнца	*sheerma u sorntsa*
axe	топор	*tupporr*

B

baby	ребёнок	*ribyonuk*
baby food	детское питание	*dyetskoyeh peetarniyeh*
baby-bottle	рожок	*ruzhork*
babysitter	няня	*nyarnya*
back (at the)	сзади	*s-zardi*
back	спина	*speenah*
backpack	станковый рюкзак	*stunkorvy ryookzark*

bad	плохой	*plukhoy*
bag	сумка	*soomka*
baker	булочная	*booluchnaya*
balcony	балкон	*bulkorn*
ball	мяч	*myach*
ballet	балет	*bullyet*
ballpoint pen	шариковая ручка	*sharikuvvaya roochka*
banana	банан	*bunnarn*
bandage	бинт	*beent*
bank (river)	берег	*byayrek*
bank pass	банковский паспорт	*barnkuffski parsspurt*
bar (café)	бар	*barr*
bar (drinks' cabinet)	бар	*barr*
barbecue	барбекю	*barbikyoo*
basketball (to play)	играть в баскетбол	*eegrart v buskitborl*
bath	ванна	*varn-na*
bath foam	пена для ванн	*pyenna dlya varn*
bath towel	банное полотенце	*barn-noye pullutyentseh*
bathing cap	купальная шапочка	*kooparlnaya sharpuchka*
bathing cubicle	раздевалка	*ruzdivarlka*
bathing suit	купальник	*kooparlnik*
bathroom	ванная	*varn-naya*
battery	батарейка	*butturryayka*
battery	аккумулятор	*akoomoolyartur*
beach	пляж	*plyash*
beans (white)	бобы (белые)	*bubby (byely-yeh)*
beautiful	красивый	*krusseevy*
beautiful	прекрасный	*prikrarsny*
beauty parlour	косметический салон	*kussmeteecheski sullorn*
bed	кровать	*kruvvart*
bedbug	клоп	*klorp*
bee	пчела	*pchillar*
beef	говядина	*guvvyardina*
beer	пиво	*peeva*
beetroot	свёкла	*svyokla*
begin	начать	*nuchart*
beginner	новичок	*nuvvichork*
behind	за	*zah*
below	внизу	*vneezoo*
belt	пояс	*por-yus*
belt	ремень	*rimyen*
bench	скамейка	*skummyayka*
berth	спальное место	*sparlnoye myesta*
better	лучше	*loochsha*
bicycle	велосипед	*villussipyet*
bicycle pump	велосипедный насос	*villussipyedny nussorss*
bicycle repairs	ремонт велосипедов	*rimornt villussipyeduff*
bikini	бикини	*beekeeni*
bill	счёт	*shchot*
billiards (to play)	играть в бильярд	*eegrart vbilyart*
birthday	день рождения	*dyen ruzhdyayniya*
birthday party	именины	*eemineeny*
biscuit	бисквит	*beeskveet*
bite	укусить	*ookoosseet*
bitter	горький	*gorki*
black	чёрный	*chorny*
bland	безвкусный	*byesfkoosny*

blanket	одеяло	*uddiyarla*
bleach (vb)	обесцветить	*ubbyestvyeteet*
blister	волдырь	*vuldyr*
block of flats	многоэтажный дом	*mnorga-etarzny dorm*
blonde	белокурый	*byelokoory*
blood	кровь	*krorv*
blood pressure	давление крови	*duvvlyayniyeh krorvi*
blouse	блуза	*blooza*
blow dry	сушить феном	*soosheet fyenum*
blue	синий	*seeni*
blunt	тупой	*toopoy*
boat	лодка	*lortka*
body	тело	*tyela*
body milk	молочко	*mulluchkor*
boiled	варёный	*vurryony*
boiled ham	окорок	*orkurruk*
bonnet	капот	*kupport*
book (vb)	зарезервировать	*zarezairvee-ruvvart*
book	книга	*kneega*
book, order (vb)	заказать	*zukkuzzart*
booked	заказанный	*zukkarzunny*
booking office	билетная касса	*beelyetnaya karssa*
bookshop	книжный магазин	*kneezhny mugguzzeen*
border	граница	*grunneetsa*
bored (to be)	скучать	*skoochart*
boring	скучный	*skooshny*
born	рождённый	*ruzhdyonny*
boss	начальник	*nucharlnik*
botanical gardens	ботанический сад	*botaneecheski sart*
both	оба	*orba*
bottle	бутылка	*bootylka*
box (in theatre)	ложа	*lorzha*
box	коробка	*kurrorpka*
boy	мальчик	*marlchik*
bra	лифчик	*leefchik*
bracelet	браслет	*brusslyet*
braised	тушёный	*tooshony*
brake	тормоз	*tormuss*
brake fluid	тормозная жидкость	*turmuznahya zhitkust*
bread	хлеб	*khlyep*
break (leg)	сломать (ногу)	*slummart (norgoo)*
breakdown	неисправность	*nyeh-eesprarvnust*
breakfast	завтрак	*zarftruk*
breast	грудь	*groot*
bridge	мост	*morst*
briefs	трусы	*troossy*
bring	принести	*preenistee*
broadcast	передача	*piridarcha*
brochure	брошюра	*brushoora*
broken	сломанный	*slormunny*
broth	бульон	*boolyorn*
brother	брат	*brart*
brown	коричневый	*kurreechnyevy*
bruise (vb)	ушибить	*ooshibeet*
brush	щётка	*shchotka*
Brussels sprouts	брюссельская капуста	*bryoosyellskaya kuppoosta*
bucket	ведро	*vidror*

building	здание	*zdarniyeh*
buoy	буй	*booy*
burglary	взлом	*vzlorm*
burn (n)	ожог	*uzhork*
burn	гореть	*gurryayt*
burnt	пригорелый	*preegurryely*
bus	автобус	*ufftorboos*
bus station	автовокзал	*arftavukkzarl*
bus stop	остановка автобуса	*ustunnorfka ufftorboosa*
business class	бизнес-класс	*beeznyess-klarss*
business trip	деловая поездка	*dyelluvvahya puyestka*
busy	занятый	*zarnyaty*
butane camping gas	бутан	*bootarn*
butcher	мясной магазин	*myassnoy mugguzzeen*
butter	масло	*marsla*
buttered roll	булочка (с маслом)	*booluchka (smarsslum)*
button	пуговица	*pooguveetsa*
button (on appliance)	кнопка	*knorpka*
buy	купить	*koopeet*

C

cabbage	капуста	*kapoosta*
cabin	каюта	*kayoota*
café	кафе	*kuff-eh*
cake	пирожное	*peerorzhnoyeh*
cake	торт	*tort*
cake shop	кондитер	*kundeetyer*
cake biscuit	печенье	*pichaynyeh*
called (to be)	меня/его/её зовут	*minya yivvor/yiyor zuvvoot*
camera	фотоаппарат	*futta-uppurrart*
camp (vb)	жить в палатке	*zhit fpullartkyeh*
camp shop	магазин	*mugguzzeen*
camp site	кемпинг	*kyempink*
camper	кемпер	*kyempyer*
campfire	костёр	*kustyor*
camping guide	путеводитель	*pootyevuddeetyel*
	по кемпингу	*puh kyempingoo*
camping permit	разрешение на кемпинг	*ruzzrishaynіyeh nah*
		kyempink
canal boat	прогулочный катер	*pruggooluchny kartyer*
cancel	аннулировать	*unnooleeruvvart*
candle	свеча	*svyichar*
canoe (vb)	грести на байдарке	*gristee nah bighdarkyeh*
canoe	байдарка	*bighdarka*
canvas	холст	*khorlst*
car	машина	*mushina*
car	вагон	*vuggorn*
car breakdown	поломка мотора	*pullormka muttora*
car deck	автомобильная палуба	*ufftummubeelnaya parlooba*
car documents	паспорт автомобиля	*parsspurt ufftummubeelya*
car trouble	неудача	*nyeoodarcha*
carafe	графин	*gruffeen*
caravan	автоприцеп/караван	*arftapreetsep/kurruhvarn*
cardigan	жилет	*zhilyet*
careful	осторожный	*usturrorzhny*
carton	блок	*blork*
cartridge	кассета	*kussyeta*

cascade	водопад	*vuddupart*
cash desk	касса	*karssa*
casino	казино	*kazeenor*
cassette	кассета	*kussyeta*
castle	замок	*zarmuk*
cat	кошка	*korshka*
catalogue	каталог	*kuttullork*
cathedral	собор	*subbor*
cauliflower	цветная капуста	*tsvitnahya kupoosta*
cave	пещера	*pishchaira*
CD	компакт-диск	*kumparkt-deesk*
celebrate	пировать	*peeruvvart*
cellotape	клейкая лента	*klyaykaya lyenta*
cemetery	кладбище	*klardbeeshcheh*
centimetre	сантиметр	*sunteemyetr*
central heating	центральное отопление	*tsentrarlnoyeh uttuplyayniyeh*
centre	в середине	*fsirideenyeh*
centre	центр	*tsentr*
chair	стул	*stool*
chambermaid	горничная	*gornichnaya*
champagne	шампанское	*shumparnskoyeh*
change (trains etc)	пересесть	*pirisyest*
change (vb)	изменить	*eezmineet*
change (money)	обменять	*ubbminyart*
change the baby's nappy	перепеленать	*piripillinart*
change the oil	сменить масло	*smineet marssla*
chapel	часовня	*chussorvnya*
charter flight	чартерный рейс	*charterny rayss*
chat up	кадрить	*kuddreet*
check	проверить	*pruvvayreet*
check in	прокомпостировать билет	*prukkumpus teeruvvat beelyet*
cheers	за здоровье	*zah zdurrorvyeh*
cheese	сыр	*syr*
chemist	аптека	*uptyeka*
cheque	чек	*chyek*
cherries	вишни	*veeshni*
chess	играть в шахматы	*eegrart vsharkhmutty*
chewing gum	жвачка	*zhvarchka*
chicken	курица	*kooritsa*
chicory	цикорий	*tsikori*
child	ребёнок	*ribyonuk*
child's car seat	детское сидение	*dyetskoye seedyayniyeh*
child's seat	детское седло	*dyetskoyeh siddlor*
chilled	прохладный	*prukhlardny*
chin	подбородок	*puddburrorduk*
chips	жареная картошка	*zharyenaya kartorshka*
chocolate	шоколад	*shokullart*
choose	выбрать	*vybrat*
chop	отбивная котлета	*utbivnaya kuttlyetta*
christian name	имя	*eemya*
church	церковь	*tsairkuf*
church service	(церковная) служба	*(tsirkorvnaya) sloozhba*
cigar	сигара	*seegara*
cigarette	сигарета	*seegurryeta*
cigarette paper	промокашка	*prummukkarshka*

ciné camera	киноаппарат	*keena-uppurr**art***
circle	круг	*krook*
circus	цирк	*tsirk*
city map	схема	*skhyema*
classical concert	классический концерт	*klass**ee**chiskee kunts**airt***
clean (vb)	почистить	*puch**ee**steet*
clean	чистый	*ch**ee**sty*
clear	ясный	*yar**sny***
clearance	уборка	*oo**bor**ka*
closed	закрытый	*zukk**ry**ty*
closed off	закрыт	*zukk**ryt***
clothes	одежда	*udd**ye**zhda*
clothes hanger	плечики	*ply**ay**chiki*
clothes peg	прищепка	*preeshch**ep**ka*
clothing	одежда	*udd**ye**zhda*
coat	пальто	*parl**tor***
cockroach	таракан	*turrukk**arn***
cocoa	какао	*kukk**ah**-oh*
cod	треска	*trisk**ar***
coffee	кофе	*kor**fyeh***
coffee filter	фильтр (для кофе)	*feeltr (dlya kor**fyeh**)*
cognac	коньяк	*kunn**yak***
cold (n)	насморк	*nars**murk***
cold	холодный	*khull**ord**ny*
cold cuts	мясные изделия	*myissny-yeh eezd**yay**liya*
collarbone	ключица	*klyooch**ee**tsa*
colleague	коллега	*kull**ye**ga*
collision	столкновение	*stulknuvv**yay**niyeh*
cologne	одеколон	*uddikull**orn***
colour	цвет	*tsvyet*
colour pencils	цветные карандаши	*tsvitny-yeh kurrun dush**ee***
colour TV	цветной телевизор	*tsvit**noy** tyelev**ee**zor*
colouring book	альбом для раскрашивания	*arl**borm** dlya raskr**ar**shivarniya*
comb	расчёска	*rasch**os**ka*
come	прийти/приехать	*preet**ee**/pree**ye**khat*
come back	вернуться	*virn**oot**sa*
complaint	жалоба	*zhar**lub**ba*
complaints book	книга жалоб	*kneega zhar**lupp***
completely	совсем	*suff**syem***
compliment	комплимент	*kumplim**yent***
compulsory	обязательный	*ubbyuzz**art**yelny*
concert	концерт	*kunts**airt***
concert hall	концертный зал	*kunts**airt**ny zarl*
concussion	сотрясение мозга	*suttryas**yay**niye **mor**zga*
condensed milk	концентрированное молоко	*kuntsentr**ee**ruvun noyeh mullukk**or***
condom	презерватив	*prezairvutt**eeff***
congratulate	поздравлять	*puzdruvv**lyart***
connection	связь	*svy**arss***
constipation	запор	*zupp**or***
consulate	консульство	*korn**sool**stva*
consultation	консультация	*kunnsoolt**art**siya*
contact lens	контактная линза	*kunnt**arkt**naya **lee**nza*
contact lens solution	жидкость для контактных линз	*zh**eet**kust dlya kunnt**arkt**nykh leens*

English	Russian	Transliteration
contagious	заразный	zurrarzny
contraceptive	противозачаточное средство	prutteevozuchar tuchnoyeh sryetstva
contraceptive pill	противозачаточные таблетки	prutteevozuchar tuchny-yeh tubblyetki
cook (vb)	готовить	guttorveet
cook	повар	porvur
copper	медь	myed
copy	копия	korpiya
corkscrew	штопор	shtorpur
corner	угол	oogul
correct	правильный	prarveelny
correspond	переписываться	piripeessyvvutsa
corridor	коридор	kurreedor
cot	детская кроватка	dyetskaya kruvvartka
cotton	хлопок	khlorpuk
cotton wool	вата	varta
cough	кашель	karshel
cough mixture	микстура от кашля	mikstoora ut karshlya
counter	окно	uknor
country	страна	strunnah
country (village)	деревня	diryevnya
country code	код страны	kort strunny
courgette	кабачок	kubbuchork
course of treatment	лечение	lichayniyeh
cousin (female)	двоюродная сестра	dvuhyoorudnaya syistrar
cousin (male)	двоюродный брат	dvuyoorudny brart
crab	краб	krarp
crayfish	рак	rark
cream	сливки	sleefki
credit card	кредитная карточка	kredeetnaya kartuchka
crisps	чипсы	cheepsy
cross-country run	лыжная трасса	lyzhnaya trarssa
cross-country skiing	кататься на лыжах	kuttartsa nah lyzhakh
cross-country skis	лыжи	lyzhi
cross the road	перейти	pireetee
crossing	переправа	piriprarva
crossing	перекрёсток	pirikryostuk
cry	плакать	plarkat
cubic metre	кубический метр	koobeecheski myetr
cucumber	огурец	uggooryets
cuddly toy	плюшевая игрушка	plyooshevaya eegrooshka
cufflinks	запонки	zarpunki
culottes	юбка-брюки	yoopka-bryooki
cup	чашка	charshka
curly	вьющийся	v-yooshchiysya
current	течение	tichayniyeh
cushion	подушечка	puddooshuchka
custard	крем	kryem
customary	обычно	ubbychna
customs	таможня	tummorzhnya
customs inspection	таможенный досмотр	tummorzhinny dusmortr
cut (vb)	резать	ryezart
cutlery	прибор	preebor

D

dairy produce	молочные продукты	*mullorchny-yeh pruddookty*
damaged	повреждённый	*puvvrizhdyonny*
dance	танцевать	*tuntsivart*
danger	опасность	*upparsnust*
dangerous	опасный	*upparsny*
dark	тёмный	*tyomny*
date (rendezvous)	встреча	*fstraycha*
daughter	дочь	*dorch*
day (hrs)	сутки	*sootki*
day	день	*dyen*
day after tomorrow	послезавтра	*porslizarftra*
day before yesterday	позавчера	*puzzufchirar*
dead	мёртвый	*myortvy*
dear (sweet)	милый	*meely*
decaffeinated	без кофеина	*byes kuffayeena*
December	декабрь	*dyekarbr*
deck chair	шезлонг	*shezlornk*
declare(customs)	предъявить на таможне	*prid-yaveet nah tummorzhneh*
deep	глубокий	*glooborki*
deep sea diving	подводное плавание	*puddvordnoyeh plarvunniyeh*
deepfrozen	замороженный	*zummurrorzhinny*
degrees	градусы	*grardoosy*
delay	задержка	*zuddyershka*
delicious	вкусный	*fkoosny*
delicious	великолепный	*vyelikullyepny*
dentist	зубной врач	*zoobnoy vrarch*
dentures	зубной протез	*zoobnoy pruttess*
deodorant	дезодорант	*dezuddurrarnt*
department	отдел	*utdyel*
department store	универмаг	*ooneevairmark*
departure	отъезд	*utt-yest*
departure time	время отправления	*vraymya utpruvvlyayniya*
depilatory cream	средство для удаления волос	*sryetstva dlya oodalyayniya vullorss*
deposit	залог	*zullork*
dessert	десерт	*dyissairt*
destination	конец маршрута	*kunnyets marshroota*
destination	назначение	*naznuchayniyeh*
develop	проявить	*pruhyuvveet*
diabetic	диабетик	*deeabbaytik*
dial	набрать	*nubbrart*
diamond	алмаз	*ullmarss*
diarrhoea	понос	*punnorss*
diarrhoea treatment	лекарство от поноса	*likarstva ut punnorssa*
dictionary	словарь	*sluvvar*
diesel	дизель	*deezil*
diesel oil	дизельное масло	*deezilnoyeh marslo*
diet	диета	*diyeta*
difficulty	сложность	*slorzhnust*
dining room	столовая	*stullorvaya*
dining/buffet car	вагон-ресторан	*vuggorn-risturrarn*
dinner (to have)	ужинать	*oozhinnart*
dinner	ужин	*oozhin*
dinner jacket	смокинг	*smorkink*

15

direct	прямой	*pryummoy*
direction	направление	*nuppruvlyayniyeh*
dirty	грязный	*gryazny*
disabled	инвалид	*eenvulleet*
disappearance	исчезновение	*eescheznuvv yayniyeh*
disco	дискотека	*deeskutyeka*
discount	скидка	*skeetka*
dish	блюдо	*blyooda*
dish of the day	дежурное блюдо	*dyezhoornoyeh blyooda*
disinfectant	дезинфицирующее средство	*dyezeenfitseerooy ooshcheh-yeh sryetstva*
distance	расстояние	*rus-stuyarniyeh*
distilled water	дистиллированная вода	*distileerorvunnaya vuddar*
disturb	помешать	*pummishart*
dive	нырять	*nyryart*
diving	водолазный спорт	*vuddullarzny sport*
diving board	трамплин	*trumpleen*
diving gear	водолазные принадлежности	*vuddullarzny-yeh preenudlyayzhnusti*
divorced	разведён (разведена)	*ruzvidyon (ruzvidyinar)*
DIY-shop	магазин «сделай сам»	*mugguzzeen "zdyelay sarm"*
dizzy	у меня кружится голова	*oo minya kroozhit sa gulluvvar*
do	делать	*dyellut*
doctor	врач	*vrarch*
dog	собака	*subbarka*
doll	кукла	*kookla*
domestically (inside country)	внутри страны	*vnootree strunny*
done (cooked)	варёный	*vurryony*
door	дверь	*dvyair*
double	двухместный	*dvookhmyestny*
draught (there is a)	сквозить	*skvuzzeet*
draughts (to play)	играть в шашки	*eegrart fsharshki*
dream	мечтать	*michtart*
dress	платье	*plartyeh*
dressing gown	халат	*khullart*
drink (n)	напиток	*nuppeetuk*
drink	пить	*peet*
drinking water	питьевая вода	*peetyivaya vuddah*
drive (vb)	ехать	*yekhat*
driver	шофёр	*shuffyor*
driving licence	водительские права	*vuddeetyelskiyeh pruvvar*
drought	засуха	*zarssookhah*
drugs	наркотики	*narkortiki*
dry	сушить	*soosheet*
dry	сухой	*sookhoy*
dry clean	почистить	*pucheesteet*
dry cleaner's	(хим)чистка	*(khim)cheestka*
dry shampoo	сухой шампунь	*sookhoy shumpoon*
dummy	пустышка	*poostyshka*
during	в течение	*ftichayniyeh*
during the day	днём	*dnyom*

Word list

15

E

ear	ухо	**oo**kha
ear nose and throat (ENT) specialist	ушной врач	**oo**shnoy vrarch
ear-ache	боль в ухе	borl v**oo**khyeh
ear-drops	ушные капли	**oo**shny-yeh karpli
early	рано	rarna
earrings	серьги	s**ya**irgee
earth	земля	zim**lyah**
earthenware	посуда	puss**oo**da
east	восток	vust**ork**
easy	лёгкий	l**yo**khki
eat	есть	yest
eczema	экзема	ek**zem**ma
eel	угорь	**oo**gur
egg	яйцо	yights**or**
elastic band	резинка	riz**ee**nka
electric	электрический	elik**tree**cheski
electricity	ток	tork
embassy	посольство	puss**or**lstva
emergency brake	запасной тормоз	zuppass**noy** tormuss
emergency exit	запасной выход	zuppass**noy** vykhut
emergency phone	аварийный телефон	avurr**ee**ny tyel**iforn**
emergency triangle	знак аварийной остановки	znark uvvur**ee**noy usttunn**or**fki
empty	пустой	poost**oy**
engaged (of telephone)	занят	z**ar**nyat
engaged	занятый	z**ar**nyaty
England	Англия	**Arn**gliya
English (adj)	английский	ung**lee**ski
Englishman	англичанин	unglich**ar**nin
Englishwoman	англичанка	unglich**ar**nka
enjoy	наслаждаться	nussluzhd**ar**tsa
envelope	конверт	kunnv**yair**t
evening (in the)	вечером	v**ay**chirum
evening	вечер	v**ay**chir
evening wear	вечерняя одежда	vich**air**nyaya udd**ye**zhda
event	событие	subb**yt**iyeh
everything	всё	fsyo
everywhere	везде	vizd**yeh**
examine	осмотреть	ussmutt**ray**t
excavation	раскопки	rask**or**pki
excellent	отличный	utt**lee**chny
exchange	обменять	ubmin**yart**
exchange office	пункт обмена валюты	poonkt ubbm**ye**na vull**yoo**ty
exchange rate	курс	k**oor**ss
excursion	экскурсия	eksk**oor**siya
exhibition	выставка	v**y**stuffka
exit	выход	v**y**khudd
expenses	расходы	russkh**or**dy
expensive	дорогой	durrugg**oy**
explain	объяснить	ubb-y**us**sneet
express train	скорый поезд	sk**or**y p**or**-yist
external	внешний	vn**ye**shni
eye	глаз	glarss
eyedrops	глазные капли	gluzz**ny**-yeh karpli

Word list

15

eyeshadow	тени (для глаз)	*tyayni (dlya glarss)*
eye specialist	глазной врач	*gluzznoy vrarch*
eyeliner	карандаш для	*kurrundarsh dlya*
	обводки глаз	*ubvortki glarss*

F

face	лицо	*leetsor*
factory	завод	*zuvvort*
fair	балаганы	*bulluggarny*
faith	вера	*vyaira*
fall	упасть	*ooparst*
family	семья	*sim-yar*
famous	знаменитый	*znammineety*
far away	далёкий	*dullyoki*
farm	ферма	*fyairma*
farmer	крестьянин	*krist-yarnin*
farmer's wife	крестьянка	*krist-yanka*
fashion	мода	*morda*
fast	быстрый	*bystry*
father	отец	*uttyets*
fault	вина	*veenar*
fax (vb)	отослать факс	*uttusslart farks*
February	февраль	*fivvrarl*
feel	чувствовать	*choostvuvvart*
feel like	хотеть	*khuttyayt*
ferry	паром	*purrorm*
fill (tooth)	пломбировать	*plumbeerruvvart*
fill out	заполнить	*zupporlneet*
filling	пломба	*plormba*
film	фильм	*feelm*
filter	фильтр	*feeltr*
find	найти	*nigh-tee*
fine	штраф	*shtrarf*
finger	палец	*parlyets*
fire	огонь	*uggorn*
fire	пожар	*puzhar*
fire brigade	пожарная команда	*puzharnaya kummarnda*
fire escape	пожарная лестница	*puzharnaya lyessnitsa*
fire extinguisher	огнетушитель	*ugnyetoosheetyel*
first	первый	*pyairvy*
first aid	скорая помощь	*skoraya pormushch*
first class	первый класс	*pyairvy klarss*
fish (vb)	ловить рыбу	*luvveet ryboo*
fish	рыба	*ryba*
fishing rod	удочка	*ooduchka*
fitness centre	спортивно- оздоровительный центр	*spurteevna-uzdur raveetyelny tsentr*
fitness training	спортивно оздоровительная тренировка	*spurteevna-uzdur raveetyelnaya tre neerorfka*
fitting room	примерочная	*preemyairuchnaya*
fix (stick together)	заклеить	*zukklyayeet*
flag	флаг	*flark*
flash	вспышка	*fspyshka*
flash bulb	лампочка для вспышки	*larmpuchka dlya fspyshki*
flea market	барахолка	*burrukhorlka*
flight	полёт	*pullyot*

flight number	рейс	*rayss*
flood	наводнение	*nuvvudnyayniyeh*
floor	пол	*porl*
floor	этаж	*etarzh*
flour	мука	*mookar*
'flu	грипп	*greep*
flyover	путепровод	*pootyehpruvvort*
fly (insect)	муха	*mookha*
fly (vb)	лететь	*lityayt*
fog	туман	*toomarn*
foggy (to be)	стоит туман	*stuh-eet toomarn*
folkloristic	фольклорный	*folklorny*
follow	последовать	*pusslyayduvvart*
food	пища	*peeshcha*
food	продукты	*pruddookty*
food poisoning	пищевое отравление	*peeshchivvor-yeh uttruvvlyayniyeh*
foot	нога	*nuggar*
for hire	сдаётся	*zdayotsa*
forbidden	запрещён	*zupprishchon*
forehead	лоб	*lorp*
foreign	иностранный	*eenustrarny*
forget	забыть	*zubbyt*
fork	вилка	*veelka*
form	бланк	*blarnk*
fort	крепость	*kryepust*
forward (vb)	переслать	*pirislart*
fountain	фонтан	*funtarn*
four-star	бензин высшего качества	*binzeen vys-shuv va karchistva*
frame	оправа	*upprarva*
franc	франк	*frarnk*
free	свободный	*svubbordny*
free (gratis)	бесплатный	*byesplartny*
free time	свободное время	*svubbordnoyeh vraymya*
freeze	морозить	*murrorzeet*
French	французский	*frunntsooski*
French bread	батон	*buttorn*
fresh	свежий	*svyayzhi*
Friday	пятница	*pyartnitsa*
fried	жареный	*zharinny*
fried egg	(яичница-)глазунья	*(ya-eeshnitsa-)gluzzoonya*
fried eggs	яичница	*ya-eeshnitsa*
friend	друг	*drook*
friendly	сердечный	*sairdyaychny*
friendly	любезный	*lyoobyezny*
frightened	боязливый	*buyazleevy*
fringe	чёлка	*cholka*
fruit	фрукты	*frookty*
fruit juice	фруктовый сок	*frooktorvy sork*
frying pan	сковорода	*skuvvurruddar*
full	полный	*porlny*
fun	удовольствие	*ooduvvorlstveeyeh*
fun	забавный	*zubbarvny*

G

gallery	галерея	*galliraya*
game	игра	*eegrar*
garage	гараж	*gurrarsh*
garbage bag	мусорный мешок	*moosorny mishork*
garden	сад	*sart*
gastroenteritis	расстройство желудка	*rus-stroystva zhilootka*
	и кишок	*ee keeshork*
gate in fence	калитка	*kulleetka*
gauze	марля	*marlya*
gel	гель	*gell*
German	немецкий	*nimyetskiy*
get hold of	достать	*dustart*
get married (m)	жениться	*zhinneetsa*
get married (f)	выйти замуж	*vytee zarmoozh*
get off	выйти	*vytee*
gift	подарок	*puddaruk*
gilt	позолоченный	*puzzullorchunny*
ginger	имбирь	*imbeer*
girl	девочка	*dyevuchka*
girlfriend	подруга	*pudrooga*
giro cheque	жироприказ	*zheeropreekarss*
giro pass	жиропас	*zheeroparss*
glacier	ледник	*lyidneek*
glass (tumbler)	стакан	*stukkarn*
glass (vodka)	рюмка	*ryoomka*
glass (wine-)	бокал	*bukkarl*
glasses (sun-)	очки	*uchkee*
glide	лететь на планёре	*lityayt nah plunnyoryeh*
glove	перчатка	*pirchartka*
glue	клей	*klyay*
gnat	комар	*kummar*
go	идти/ехать	*eed-tee/yekhat*
go back	вернуться	*virnootsa*
go out	прогуляться	*pruggoolyartsa*
goat's cheese	козий сыр	*korzee syr*
gold	золото	*zorlutta*
golf course	площадка для	*plushchartka dlya*
	игры в гольф	*eegry vgorlf*
golf stockings	гольфы	*gorlfy*
good afternoon	добрый день	*dorbry dyen*
good evening	добрый вечер	*dorbry vyaychir*
good morning	доброе утро	*dorbroye ootra*
good night	спокойной ночи	*spukkoyny norchi*
goodbye (n)	прощание	*prushcharniye*
goodbye	до свидания	*duh sveedarniya*
gram	грамм	*grarm*
grandchild	внук (внучка)	*vnook (vnoochka)*
grandfather	дедушка	*dyedooshka*
grandmother	бабушка	*barbooshka*
grape juice	виноградный сок	*veenugrardny sork*
grapefruit	грейпфрут	*graypfroot*
grapes	виноград	*veenugrart*
grave	могила	*mugeela*
greasy	жирный	*zheerny*
green	зелёный	*zillyony*
greet	здороваться	*zdurrorvatsa*

grey	серый	*syairy*
grey (of hair)	седой	*sidoy*
grill	жарить на вертеле	*zharit nah vyairtyelyeh*
grilled	жареный на вертеле	*zhariny nah vyairtyelyeh*
grocer's	бакалейный магазин	*bukkullyayny mugguzzeen*
group	группа	*groopa*
guest house	пансион	*punnseeorn*
guide (book)	путеводитель	*pootyevuddeetyel*
guide (person)	гид	*geet*
guided tour	экскурсия	*ekskoorsiya*
gynaecologist	гинеколог	*geenyekorlukk*

H

hair	волосы	*vorlussy*
hair-do	причёска	*preechoska*
hairbrush	щётка	*shchotka*
hairdresser	парикмахерская (женская мужская)	*parikmarkherskaya*
hairpins	шпильки	*shpeelki*
hairspray	лак для волос	*lark dlya vullorss*
half (advb)	наполовину	*napulluvveenoo*
half	половина	*pulluveena*
half a kilo	полкило	*pullkeelor*
half full	полупустой	*pulloopoostoy*
hammer	молоток	*mulluttork*
hand	рука	*rookar*
handbrake	ручной тормоз	*roochnoy tormuss*
handbag	сумка	*soomka*
handkerchief	носовой платок	*nussuvvoy pluttork*
handmade	сделанный вручную	*zdyelunny vroochnooyu*
happy	рад (рада)	*raht (rarda)*
harbour	порт	*port*
hard	твёрдый	*tvyordy*
hat	шляпа	*shlyarpa*
hayfever	сенная лихорадка	*syinnahya likhurratka*
hazelnut	лесной орех	*lyissnoy urryekh*
head	голова	*gulluvvar*
headache	головная боль	*gulluvnahya borl*
health	здоровье	*zdurrorvyeh*
health food shop	магазин натуральных продуктов	*mugguzzeen nut toorarlnykh*
hear	слышать	*slyshart*
hearing aid	слуховой аппарат	*slookhuvvoy uppurrart*
heart	сердце	*sairtseh*
heart patient	у него больное сердце	*oo nyivvor bullnor-yeh sairtseh*
heater	отопление	*uttuplyayniyeh*
heavy	тяжёлый	*tyuzholly*
heel	пятка	*pyartka*
heel	каблук	*kablook*
hello	здравствуйте	*zdrarstvooytyeh*
hello (colloquial)	привет	*preevyet*
helmet	шлем	*shlyem*
help (vb)	помочь	*pummorch*
help!	помощь	*pormushch*
helping	порция	*portseeya*
herbal tea	чай из трав	*chigh ees trahf*

here	здесь	zdyess
herring	селёдка	silyotka
high	высокий	vyssorki
high tide	прилив	preeleef
highchair	детский стульчик	dyetski stoolchik
hiking	пешеходный туризм	pishikhordny tooreezm
hiking trip	поход	pukhort
hip	бедро	byidror
hire	снять	snyat
hitchhike	путешествовать автостопом	pootyeshestvuvvart arftostorpum
hobby	хобби	khorbi
hold-up	налёт	nullyot
holiday	отпуск	ortpoosk
holiday house	дача	darcha
home (at)	дома	dorma
homesickness	тоска по родине	tusskar puh rordeenyeh
honest	честный	chaystny
honey	мёд	myot
honeydew melon	дыня	dynya
horizontal	горизонтальный	gurreezuntarlny
horrible	отвратительный	utvrateetyulny
horse	лошадь	lorshut
hospital	больница	bullneetsa
hospitality	гостеприимство	gostipree-eemstva
hot-water bottle	грелка	gryelka
hotel	гостиница	gusteenitsa
hour	час	charss
house	дом	dorm
household items	хозяйственные товары	khuzyigh-stvunny-yeh tuvvary
houses of parliament	здание парламента	zdarniyeh parlarmyenta
housewife	домохозяйка	dormakhuzzyighka
how far?	как далеко?	kukk dullikor?
how long?	как долго?	kukk dorlga?
how much?	сколько?	skorlka?
how?	как?	kark?
hundred grams	сто грамм	stor grarm
hunger	голод	gorlut
hurricane	ураган	ooruggarn
hurry (n)	поспешность	puspyeshnust
husband	муж	moozh
hut	избушка	eezbooshka
hyperventilation	гипервентиляция	geeperventeelyatsiya

I

ice cubes	кубики льда	koobeeki l-dah
ice skates	коньки	kunkee
ice-cream	мороженое	murrorzhinoyeh
idea	идея	eedyaya
identification	удостоверение личности	oodustuvviryayniyeh leechnusti
identify	установить личность	oostunnuvveet leechnust
ignition key	ключ зажигания	klyooch zuzhigarniya
ill	больной	bullnoy
illness	болезнь	bullyezn

Word list

15

130

imagine	представить себе	*pridstarveet sibbyeh*
immediately	непосредственный	*nyehpussraydstvinny*
import duty	пошлина	*porshlina*
impossible	невозможный	*nyehvuzzmorzhny*
in	в	*v*
in front of	перед	*pyayrut*
included	включая	*fklyoochahya*
indicate	показать	*pukkuzzart*
indicator	указатель поворота	*ookuzzartyel puvvurrorta*
inexpensive	дешёвый	*dishorvy*
infection	заражение	*zurruzhayniyeh*
inflammation	воспаление	*vusspullyayniyeh*
information	информация	*eenformartsiyah*
information office	справочное бюро	*sprarvuchnoyeh byooror*
injection	укол	*ookorl*
injured	раненый	*rarnyunny*
inner tube	камера шины	*karmyera shiny*
innocent	невинный	*nyehveeny*
insect	насекомое	*nussikormoye*
insect bite	укус насекомого	*ookoos nussikormuvva*
insect repellant	масло против комаров	*marslo prorteef kummarorff*
inside	внутри	*vnootree*
insole	стелька	*styelka*
instructions	правила пользования	*prarveela porlzuvvunniya*
insurance	страхование	*strukhuvvarniyeh*
intermission	перерыв	*piriryff*
international	международный	*myezhdoonurrordny*
interpreter	переводчик	*pirivortchik*
introduce oneself	представиться	*pridstarveetsa*
invite	пригласить	*preeglusseet*
iodine	йод	*yot*
Ireland	Ирландия	*Eerlarndeeya*
Irish (adj)	ирландский	*eerlarnski*
Irishman	ирландец	*eerlarndyets*
Irishwoman	ирландка	*eerlarntka*
iron	железо	*zhilyayza*
iron	гладить	*glardeet*
iron (metal)	утюг	*ootyook*
ironing board	гладильная доска	*gluddeelnaya duskar*
island	остров	*orstruff*
Italian	итальянский	*eetullyarnski*
itch	зуд	*zoot*

J

jack	домкрат	*dumkrart*
jacket	пиджак	*pidzhark*
January	январь	*yunvar*
jaw	челюсть	*chaylyoost*
jeans	джинсы	*dzheenssy*
jellyfish	медуза	*midooza*
jeweller	ювелир	*yooveleer*
jewellery	драгоценности	*draggotsenusti*
jog	бегать	*byegart*
joke	шутка	*shootka*
juice	сок	*sork*
July	июль	*eeyool*
jumble sale	барахолка	*burrakhorlka*

jump leads	электропровод (для присоединения к аккумулятору другой машины)	*elektroprorvut (dlya preesuhyid inyayniya kukkoo moolyah-turroo droogoy mushiny)*
jumper	свитер	*sveeter*
June	июнь	*eeyoon*

K

key	ключ(ик)	*klyooch(ik)*
kilo	кило	*keelor*
kilometre	километр	*keelommyetr*
king	король	*kurrorl*
kiss (vb)	целовать	*tsilluvvart*
kiss	поцелуй	*putsilooy*
kitchen	кухня	*kookhnya*
knee	колено	*kullyayno*
knickers	трусики	*troosikki*
knife	нож	*norsh*
knit	вязать	*vyazart*
know	знать	*znart*

L

lace	кружево	*kroozhivva*
ladies'	женский туалет	*zhenski tooullyet*
lake	озеро	*orzira*
lamp	лампа	*larmpa*
land	приземлиться	*preezimleetsa*
lane	полоса движения	*pullussar dveezhayniya*
language	язык	*yuzzyk*
lard	сало	*sarlo*
large	большой	*bullshoy*
last (previous)	прошлый	*prorshly*
last	последний	*puslaydni*
last night	прошлой ночью	*prorshloy norchyoo*
late	поздний	*porzni*
later	потом	*puttorm*
laugh (vb)	смеяться	*smeeyartsa*
launderette	прачечная	*prarchichnaya*
law	право	*prarvo*
laxative	слабительное	*slabeetyelnoyeh*
leather	кожа	*korzha*
leather goods	кожевенные товары	*kuzhevin-ny-yeh tuvvary*
leave	уехать	*ooyekhat*
leek	порей	*purray*
left (on the)	налево	*nahlyeva*
left	левый	*lyevy*
left luggage	камера хранения багажа	*karmyera khrun-nyayniya bugguzhar*
leg	нога	*nuggar*
lemon	лимон	*leemorn*
lend	дать взаймы	*dart vzigh-my*
lens	линза	*leenza*
lentils	чечевица	*chichiveetsa*
less	меньше	*myensha*
lesson	урок	*oorork*
letter	письмо	*peessmor*

lettuce	кочанный салат	*kucharn-ny sullart*
level crossing	железнодорожный переезд	*zhileyeznodur rorzhny pireeyest*
library	библиотека	*beebliotyeka*
lie (tell lies)	лгать	*l-gart*
lie	лежать	*lizhart*
lift (hitchhike)	подвезти	*puddvistee*
lift (in building)	лифт	*leeft*
lift (ski)	кресельная канатная дорога	*kraysyelnaya kunnartnaya durrorga*
light (n)	свет	*svyet*
light (not dark)	светлый	*svyetly*
light (not heavy)	лёгкий	*lyokhki*
lighter	зажигалка	*zuzhigarlka*
lighthouse	маяк	*mayark*
lightning	молния	*morlniya*
like (I like it)	мне нравится	*mnyeh nrarvitsa*
like/love	любить	*lyoobeet*
line	линия	*leeneeya*
lipstick	губная помада	*goobnahya pummarda*
liquorice	лакрица	*lukkreetsa*
listen	слушать	*slooshat*
literature	литература	*litairatoora*
litre	литр	*leetr*
little (a)	немного	*nimnorga*
live	жить	*zhit*
live together	жить совместно	*zhit suvvmyestna*
local	местный	*myestny*
lock	замок	*zummork*
long	длинный	*dleeny*
look (vb)	смотреть	*smuttrayt*
look for	искать	*eeskart*
look round	осмотреть	*ussmuttrayt*
lorry	грузовик	*groozuvveek*
lose	потерять	*puttyiryart*
loss	потеря	*puttyairya*
lost (to be)	заблудиться	*zubbloodeetsa*
lost	потерянный	*puttyayryunny*
lost item	пропажа	*pruparzha*
lost property office	находки	*nukhortki*
lotion	лосьон	*luss-yon*
loud	громко	*grormka*
love (to be in - with)	влюблён (влюблена)	*vlyooblyon (vlyooblinar)*
love	любовь	*lyooborf*
low	низкий	*neeski*
low tide	отлив	*uttleef*
liquid petrolium gas	сжиженный (нефтяной) газ	*s-zhizhunny (nyeftyanoy) garss*
luck	счастье	*scharstyah*
luggage	багаж	*buggarzh*
luggage locker	багажная ячейка	*buggarzhnaya yachayka*
lumps of sugar	кусочки сахара	*koosorchki sarkhurra*
lunch	обед	*ubbyet*
lungs	лёгкие	*lyokhkeeyeh*

Word list

15

M

macaroni	макароны	*makkurorny*
machine (vending)	автомат	*ufftummart*
madam	госпожа	*gusspuzhar*
magazine	журнал	*zhoornarl*
mail	почта	*porchta*
main post office	главный почтамт	*glarvny puchtarmt*
main road	магистраль	*muggistrarl*
make an appointment	назначить свидание	*nuzznarcheet sveedarniyeh*
makeshift	временный	*vrayminny*
man	мужчина	*mooshcheena*
manager	заведующий	*zuvvyaydooyushchi*
mandarin	мандарин	*mundurreen*
manicure	маникюр	*munneekyoor*
map	карта	*karta*
map	географическая карта	*geogruffeecheskaya karta*
marble	мрамор	*mrarmur*
March	март	*mart*
margarine	маргарин	*margurreen*
marina	яхт-клуб	*yakht-kloop*
market	рынок	*rynuk*
marriage	брак	*brark*
married	женатый (замужем)	*zhinnarty (zarmoozhum)*
mass (church service)	обедня	*ubyednya*
massage	массаж	*mas-sarzh*
match (competition)	соревнование	*surrevnuvvarniyeh*
matches	спички	*speechki*
matt	матовый	*martuvvy*
May	май	*migh*
maybe	может быть	*morzhit byt*
mayonnaise	майонез	*migh-yoness*
mayor	мэр	*mair*
meal	еда	*yiddah*
mean(vb)	значить	*znarcheet*
meat	мясо	*myarssa*
mechanical help	техпомощь	*tyekhpormushch*
media	мидия	*meediya*
medication	лекарство	*likarstva*
medicine	лекарство	*likarstva*
meet (for first time)	познакомиться	*puznukkormitsa*
membership	членство	*chlyenstva*
menstruate (vb)	у меня менструация	*oo minya menstrooartsiya*
menstruation	менструация	*menstrooartsiya*
menu	меню	*minyoo*
menu of the day	суточное меню	*sootuchnoyeh minyoo*
message	сообщение	*suh-ubbshchayniyeh*
metal	металл	*myitarl*
meter (appliance)	счётчик	*shchotchik*
metre	метр	*myetr*
migraine	мигрень	*meegryen*
mild (tobacco)	лёгкий	*lyokhki*
milk	молоко	*mullukor*
millimetre	миллиметр	*meeleemyetr*
milometer	дистанционный спидометр	*distarntsiorny speedormyetr*
mince	рубленое мясо	*rooblyunor-yeh myarssa*
mineral water	минеральная вода	*meenirarlnaya vuddar*

minute	минута	*minoota*
mirror	зеркало	*zyairkulla*
miss (vb)	пропустить	*pruppoosteet*
missing (to be)	не хватать	*nyeh khvuttart*
mistake	ошибка	*ushipka*
mistaken (to be)	ошибиться	*ushibbeetsa*
misunderstanding	недоразумение	*nyedurrazoomyayniyeh*
modern art	современное искусство	*suvrimmyen-noyeh eeskoostva*
moment	мгновение	*m-gnuvvayniya*
monastery	монастырь	*monnustyr*
Monday	понедельник	*punnidyelnik*
money	деньги	*dyengi*
month	месяц	*myaysits*
moped	мопед	*muppyet*
morning	утро	*ootra*
morning (in the)	утром	*ootrum*
mosque	мечеть	*michayt*
motel	мотель	*muttayl*
mother	мать	*mart*
moto-cross	заниматься мотокроссом	*zannimartsa muttakrorssum*
motorbike	мотоцикл	*muttatsikl*
motorboat	моторная лодка	*muttornaya lortka*
motorway	автострада	*ufftustrarda*
mountain	гора	*gurrar*
mountain hut	хижина в горах	*kheezhina vgurrahkh*
mountain-skiing	горнолыжный спорт	*gornullyzhny sport*
mountaineering shoes	горные ботинки	*gorny-yeh butteenki*
mouse	мышь	*mysh*
mouth	рот	*rort*
much/many	много	*mnorga*
multi-storey car park	гараж (для стоянки автомобилей)	*gurrarzh (dlya stuyarnki*
muscle	мышца	*myshtsa*
muscle spasms	мышечная судорога	*myshechnaya soodurrugga*
museum	музей	*moozyay*
mushrooms	грибы	*greeby*
music	музыка	*moozyka*
musical (n)	мюзикл	*myoozikl*
mustard	горчица	*gurcheetsa*

N

nail (on finger)	ноготь	*norgut*
nail	гвоздь	*gvorsst*
nail file	пилочка для ногтей	*peeluchka dlya nukhtyay*
nail polish remover	жидкость для снятия лака (с ногтей)	*zhitkust dlya snyartiya*
nail scissors	ножницы для ногтей	*norzhneetsy dlya nukhtyay*
naked	голый	*gorly*
nappy	пелёнка	*pilyonka*
nationality	национальность	*nutsionarlnust*
naturally	конечно	*kunnyeshna*
nature	природа	*preerorda*
naturism	нудизм	*noodeezm*
nauseous	меня тошнит	*minya tushneet*
near	близко	*bleeska*

nearby	близкий	*bleeski*
necessary	необходимый	*nyeh-ubbkhud deemy*
neck	шея	*shay-ya*
necklace	цепь	*tsep*
needle	игла	*eeglar*
negative	негатив	*nyegutteef*
neighbours	соседи	*sussyedi*
nephew	племянник	*plimyahnik*
never	никогда	*neekugdar*
new	новый	*norvy*
news	новость	*norvust*
news stand	киоск	*keeorsk*
newspaper	газета	*guzzyetta*
next	следующий	*slyaydooyushchi*
next to	возле	*vorzlyeh*
nice (friendly)	милый	*meely*
nice	прекрасно	*prikrarssna*
nice to eat	вкусный	*fkoosny*
niece	племянница	*plimyarnitsa*
night	ночь	*norch*
night duty	ночная смена	*nuchnaya smyena*
nightclub	ночной клуб	*nuchnoy kloop*
nightlife	ночная жизнь	*nuchnaya zhizn*
no one	никто	*neektor*
no	нет	*nyet*
no overtaking	обгон запрещён	*ubgorn zupprishchon*
noise	шум	*shoom*
nonstop	непрерывно	*nipreeryvna*
normal	обычный	*ubbychny*
normal	нормальный	*narmarlny*
north	север	*sayvir*
nose	нос	*norss*
nose drops	капли в нос	*karpli vnorss*
nosebleed	кровотечение из носа	*krorvotichayniyeh eess norsa*
notepaper	почтовая бумага	*porchtorvaya boomarga*
nothing	ничего	*nichivvor*
November	ноябрь	*nayarbr*
now	сейчас	*siycharss*
nowhere	нигде	*neegdyeh*
nudist beach	пляж нудистов	*plyarsh noodeestuff*
number	номер	*normer*
number plate	номерной знак	*nummyernoy znark*
nurse	медсестра	*myetsistrar*
nutmeg	мускатный орех	*mooskartny urryekh*
nuts	орехи	*urryekhi*

o

October	октябрь	*uktyarbr*
off-licence	винный магазин	*veen-ny mugguzzeen*
off (food)	испорченный	*eesporchinny*
offer	предложить	*pridluzhit*
office	контора	*kuntora*
oil	масло	*marssla*
oil level	уровень масла	*ooruvvin marssla*
ointment	мазь	*marss*

ointment for burns	мазь от ожога	*marss ut uzhorga*
okay	ладно	*lardna*
old	старый	*stary*
olive oil	оливковое масло	*ulleefkuvvoyeh marssla*
olives (green)	оливки	*ulleefki*
omelette	омлет	*umlyet*
on	на	*nah*
on board	иа борту	*nah bortoo*
on the way	в пути	*fpootee*
oncoming car	встречный автомобиль	*fstraychny ufftamubbeel*
one-way traffic	одностороннее движение	*udnusturrornyeyeh dveezhayniye*
onion	лук	*look*
open (adj)	открытый	*utkryty*
open (vb)	открыть	*utkryt*
opera	опера	*orpira*
operate	оперировать	*uppaireeruvvat*
operator (telephone)	телефонистка	*tyelifunneestka*
operetta	оперетта	*uppiretta*
opposite	напротив	*nupprorteef*
optician	оптик	*orptik*
or	или	*eeli*
orange	оранжевый	*urrarnzhivy*
orange	апельсин	*uppyelseen*
orange juice	апельсиновый сок	*uppyelseenuvvy sork*
order (in -) tidy	в порядке	*fpurryatkyeh*
order (n)	заказ	*zukkarss*
order (vb)	заказать	*zukkuzzart*
other	другие	*droogee-yeh*
other side	другая сторона	*droogahya sturrunnar*
outside	вне	*vnyeh*
over the phone	по телефону	*puh tyelifornoo*
overtake	обогнать	*ubbugnart*
oysters	устрицы	*oostritsy*

P

packed lunch	сухой паёк	*sookhoy puhyok*
page	страница	*strunneetsa*
pain	боль	*borl*
painkiller	болеутоляющее средство	*borlye-ootullyahy ooshcheyeh sryetstvo*
paint	краска	*krarska*
painting (art)	живопись	*zhivuppeess*
painting (object)	картина	*karteena*
palace	дворец	*dvurryets*
pan	кастрюля	*kustryoolya*
pancake	блин	*bleen*
pane	стекло	*styiklor*
paper	бумага	*boomarga*
paper napkin	бумажная салфетка	*boomarzhnaya sulfyetka*
paraffin oil	керосин	*kyerusseen*
parasol	зонтик	*zorntik*
parcel	посылка	*pussylka*
parcel	пакет	*pukkyet*
pardon	извините	*eezveeneetyeh*
parents	родители	*rudeetyeli*
park	парк	*park*

park	поставить машину	pustarveet mushinoo
parking space	стоянка (автомобилей)	stuyarnka (uffta mubbeelyay)
parsley	петрушка	pitrooshka
partner	партнёр	partnyor
party	вечеринка	vyechereenka
passable	проходимый	prukhuddeemy
passenger	пассажир	pussuzheer
passport	паспорт	parsspurt
passport photo	фотокарточка	futtakartuchka
patient	пациент	patseeyent
patronymic	отчество	ortchistvo
pavement	тротуар	truttoo-ar
pay	платить	plutteet
pay the bill	рассчитаться	ras-schitartsa
peach	персик	pyairseek
peanuts	земляные орехи	zimlyayny-yeh urryekhi
pear	груша	grooshar
peas	(зелёный) горошек	(zillyonny) gurrorshik
pedal	педаль	piddarl
pedestrian crossing	пешеходный переход	pishikhordny pirrikhort
pedicure	педикюр	pyeddikyoor
pen	ручка	roochka
pencil	карандаш	kurrundarsh
penis	пенис	pyeniss
pepper	перец	pyayrits
performance	театральное представление	tee-uttrarlnoyeh pridstuvvlyayniyeh
perfume	духи	dookhee
perm (verb)	сделать завивку	zdyelat zuvveefkoo
perm	(химическая) завивка	(khimeecheskaya) zuvveefka
permit	разрешение	ruzzrishayniyeh
person	человек	chilluvvyek
personal	личный	leechny
petrol	бензин	byenzeen
petrol station	бензостанция	byenzustarntsiya
pets	домашние животные	dummarshniyeh zhivortny-yeh
pharmacy	аптека	uptyeka
phone (tele-)	телефон	tyeliforn
phone (vb)	позвонить	puzzvunneet
phone box	телефонная будка	tyeliforn-naya bootka
phone directory	телефонная книга	tyeliforn-naya kneega
phone number	телефонный номер	tyeliforn-ny normer
photo	снимок	sneemuk
photocopier	ксерокс	ksyairuks
photocopy (n)	фотокопия	futtakorpiya
photocopy (vb)	делать фотокопию	dyelat futtakorpiyu
pick up	забрать	zubbrart
picnic	пикник	peekneek
pictures (to take)	фотографировать	futtagruffeeruvvat
piece of clothing	предмет одежды	pridmyet uddyezhdy
pier	мол	morl
pigeon	голубь	gorloop
pill (contraceptive)	противозачаточная таблетка	prutteevuzzuchar tuchnaya tubblyetka

pillow	подушка	*puddooshka*
pillowcase	наволочка	*narvulluchka*
pin	булавка	*boolarfka*
pineapple	ананас	*unnunarss*
pipe	трубка	*troopka*
pipe tobacco	трубочный табак	*troobuchny tubbark*
pity	жаль	*zharl*
place of entertainment	место для развлечений	*myesta dlya ruzzvlichayni*
place of interest	достопримечательность	*dustupprimichartyelnust*
plan	план	*plarn*
plant	растение	*rustyayniyeh*
plasters	пластыри	*plarstyri*
plastic	пластмасса	*plustmarssa*
plastic bag	пакет	*pukkyet*
plate	тарелка	*turryelka*
platform	платформа	*pluttforma*
play	пьеса	*pyessa*
play	играть	*eegrart*
play golf	играть в гольф	*eegrart vgorlf*
playground	детская площадка	*dyetskaya plushchartka*
playing cards	(игральные) карты	*(eegrarlny-yeh) karty*
pleasant	приятный	*preeyartny*
please	пожалуйста	*puzharlooysta*
pleasure	удовольствие	*ooduvvorlstviyeh*
plum	слива	*sleeva*
pocketknife	складной нож	*skluddnoy norsh*
point (vb)	показать	*pukkuzzart*
poison	яд	*yart*
police	милиция	*meeleetsiya*
police station	отделение милиции	*utdilyayniyeh meeleetsii*
policeman	милиционер	*mileetseeonyair*
pond	пруд	*proot*
pony	пони	*porni*
pop concert	поп-концерт	*popkuntsairt*
population	население	*nussilyayniya*
pork	свинина	*sveeneena*
port (drink)	портвейн	*purrtvayn*
porter	носильщик	*nusseelshchik*
porter	швейцар	*shvaytsar*
post	почта	*porchta*
post code	почтовый индекс	*porchtorvy eendeks*
postage	почтовый сбор	*porchtorvy zbor*
postbox	почтовый ящик	*puchtorvy yashchik*
postcard	открытка	*utkrytka*
postman	почтальон	*porchtalyorn*
potato	картофель	*kartorfil*
poultry	птица	*pteetsa*
powdered milk	порошковое молоко	*purushkorvoyeh mullukkor*
power point	розетка	*ruzzyetka*
pram	детская коляска	*dyetskaya kullyarska*
prawns	креветки	*krevvyetki*
precious	дорогой	*durruggoy*
prefer	предпочесть	*pridpuchayst*
preference	предпочтение	*pridpuchtyayniyeh*
pregnant	беременная	*biryayminnaya*
present	присутствующий	*preesootstvooyushchi*

present	подарок	*puddaruk*
preserves	варенье	*varyaynyeh*
press (vb)	нажать	*nuzhart*
pressure	давление	*duvvlyayniyeh*
price	цена	*tsinar*
price list	указатель цен	*ookuzzartyel tsen*
print (vb)	печатать	*pichartat*
print	отпечаток	*utpichartuk*
probably	наверно	*nuvvyairna*
problem	проблема	*prubblyema*
profession	профессия	*pruffaysseeya*
programme	программа	*pruggrarma*
pronounce	произнести	*pruh-eeznisstee*
propane camping gas	пропан	*prupparn*
pudding	пудинг	*poodink*
pull	удалить	*oodulleet*
pull a muscle	растянуть мышцу	*rasstyannoot myshtsoo*
pulse	пульс	*poolss*
punctually	во время	*vorvraymya*
puncture	лопнула шина	*lorpnoola shina*
pure	чистый	*cheesty*
purple	лиловый	*leelorvy*
purse	кошелёк	*kushilyok*
push	толкать	*tulkart*
puzzle	головоломка	*gulluvvalormka*
pyjamas	пижама	*peezharma*

Q

quarter	четверть	*chaytvirt*
quarter of an hour	четверть часа	*chaytvirt chussar*
queen	королева	*kurrullyevva*
question	вопрос	*vupprorss*
quick	быстрый	*bystry*
quiet	спокойный	*spukkoyny*

R

radio	радио	*rahdeeo*
railway	железная дорога	*zhilyeznaya durrorga*
rain	дождь	*dorsht*
raincoat	плащ	*plarshch*
raining	идёт дождь	*eedyot dorsht*
raisins	изюм	*eezyoom*
rape	изнасилование	*eeznusseeluvvarneeyeh*
rapids	быстрина	*bystrinar*
raspberries	малина	*mulleena*
raw	сырой	*syroy*
raw ham	ветчина	*vitchinnar*
raw vegetables	сырые овощи	*syry-yeh orvushchi*
razor blades	(бритвенные) лезвия	*(breetvinny-yeh) lyayzviya*
read	читать	*chitart*
ready	готовый	*guttorvy*
really	собственно	*sorpstvinna*
receipt	квитанция	*kveetarntsiya*
receipt	справка (об уплате)	*sprarfka (ubb ooplartyeh)*
receipt	чек	*chyek*
recipe	рецепт	*ritsept*
reclining chair	шезлонг	*shezlornk*

recommend	рекомендовать	*rekummyenduvvart*
rectangle	прямоугольник	*pryarmmuh-oogorlnik*
red	красный	*krarssny*
red wine	красное вино	*krarsnoyeh veenor*
reduction	скидка	*skeetka*
refrigerator	холодильник	*khulludeelnik*
regards	привет	*preevyet*
region	область	*orblust*
registered	заказной	*zukkuzznoy*
reliable	надёжный	*nuddyozhny*
religion	религия	*releegiya*
rent out	сдать (внаём)	*zdart (vnayom)*
repair (vb)	починить	*puchinneet*
repairs	ремонт	*rimornt*
repeat	повторить	*pufturreet*
report	протокол	*pruttukkorl*
resent	обижаться	*ubbeezhartsa*
responsible	ответственный	*utvyetstvunny*
rest	отдохнуть	*utdukhnoot*
restaurant	ресторан	*risturrarn*
result	результат	*ryezooltart*
retired	пенсия	*pyensiya*
retired	на пенсии	*nah pyensii*
return (ticket)	(билет) туда и обратно	*(beelyet) toodar ee ubbrartno*
reverse (vehicle)	ехать задним ходом	*yekhat zardnim khordum*
rheumatism	ревматизм	*rivmutteezm*
rice	рис	*reess*
ridiculous	ерунда	*yiroondar*
riding (horseback)	ездить на лошади	*yezdeet nah lorshudi*
riding school	манеж	*munnyesh*
right	правый	*prarvy*
right (on the)	направо	*nupprarva*
right of way	преимущество	*prayimooshchistva*
ring (on telephone)	позвонить	*puzzvunneet*
ripe	зрелый	*zryelly*
risk	риск	*reesk*
river	река	*rikkar*
road	дорога	*durrorga*
roadway	дорога	*durorga*
roasted	жареный	*zharinny*
rock	скала	*skullar*
roll	булочка	*booluchka*
roof rack	империал	*eempereearl*
room	комната	*kormnutta*
room number	номер	*normer*
room service	обслуживание в номере	*ubbsloozhivarniyeh vnormeryeh*
root	корень	*korin*
rope	верёвка	*viryoffka*
rose	роза	*rorza*
rosé wine	розовое вино	*rorzuvvoyeh veenor*
roundabout	площадь с круговым движением	*plorshchud skrooguvvym*
route	маршрут	*marshroot*
rowing boat	гребная лодка	*gribnahya lortka*
rubber	резина	*ryezeena*

15

rubbish	ерунда	*yiroondar*
rucksack	рюкзак	*ryookzark*
rude	невежливый	*nyehvyayzhlivy*
ruins	развалины	*ruzvarleeny*
run into	встретить	*fstrayteet*

S

sad	грустный	*groosny*
safari	сафари	*suffari*
safe	безопасный	*byezupparssny*
safe	сейф	*sayf*
safety pin	английская булавка	*ungleeskaya boolarfka*
sail (vb)	плавать	*plarvat*
sailing boat	парусная лодка	*paroosnaya lortka*
salad	салат	*sullart*
salad oil	растительное масло	*rasteetyelnaya marsslo*
salami	салями	*sullyarmi*
sale	распродажа	*russpruhdarzha*
salt	соль	*sorl*
same	то же самое	*tor zhe sarmoyeh*
sandy beach	песчаный пляж	*pishcharny plyash*
sanitary pad	гигиеническая прокладка	*geegeeyeneech eskaya prukklartka*
sardines	сардины	*sardeeny*
satisfied	довольный	*duvorlny*
Saturday	суббота	*sooborta*
sauce	соус	*sor-ooss*
sauna	сауна	*sahoona*
sausage	колбаса	*kullbussar*
savoury	солёный	*sullyony*
say	сказать	*skuzzart*
scarf	шарф	*sharf*
scenic walk	прогулка по городу	*pruggoolka puh goruddoo*
school	школа	*shkorla*
scissors	ножницы	*norzhneetsy*
scooter	мотороллер	*muttaroriler*
scorpion	скорпион	*skurpeeorn*
Scotland	Шотландия	*shuttlarndiya*
Scots (adj)	шотландский	*shutlarnski*
Scotsman	шотландец	*shuttlarndits*
Scotswoman	шотландка	*shuttlarntka*
screw	винт	*veent*
screwdriver	отвёртка	*utvyortka*
sculpture	скульптура	*skoolptoora*
sea	море	*moryeh*
seasick	его укачало	*yivvor ookucharla*
seasoning	приправа	*preeprarva*
seat	место	*myesta*
second (n)	секунда	*sikkoonda*
second	второй	*fturroy*
secretion (of fluid etc)	выделение	*vydelyayniye*
sedative	успокаивающее средство	*uspukkaheevay ooshchiye sraytstva*
see	осматривать	*usmartreevart*
self-timer	автоспуск	*ufftaspoosk*
send	отправить	*uttprarveet*
sentence	предложение	*pridluzhayniyeh*

September	сентябрь	*sintyarbr*
serious	серьёзный	*siryozny*
service	обслуживание	*ubsloozhivarniyeh*
serviette	салфетка	*sulfyetka*
set (hair)	сделать завивку	*zdyelart zuvveefku*
sewing thread	швейные нитки	*shvayny-yeh neetkee*
shade	тень	*tyen*
shallow	мелкий	*myelki*
shammy	замша	*zarmsha*
shampoo	шампунь	*shampoon*
shark	акула	*ukkoola*
shave (vb)	побрить	*pubbreet*
shaver	электробритва	*ellektrobreetva*
shaving cream	крем для бритвы	*kryem dlya breetyah*
shaving soap	мыло для бритвы	*mylo dlya breetyar*
sheet	простыня	*prustynyah*
sherbet	шербет	*shirbyet*
sherry	херес	*khay-ress*
shirt	рубашка	*roobarshka*
shoe	туфля	*tooflya*
shoe polish	гуталин	*gootulleen*
shoe repairs	ремонт обуви	*rimornt orboovi*
shoe shop	обувной магазин	*ubboovnoy mugguzzeen*
shoelace	шнурок	*shnoorork*
shop (vb)	делать покупки	*dyelat pukoopki*
shop	магазин	*mugguzzeen*
shop assistant	продавщица	*pruddafshcheetsa*
shop window	витрина	*vitreena*
shopping centre	торговый центр	*turrgorvy tsentr*
short	короткий	*kurrortki*
short circuit	короткое замыкание	*kurrortkoyeh zum mykarniyeh*
shorts	шорты	*shorty*
shoulder	плечо	*plichor*
show	шоу	*shoroo*
shower	душ	*doosh*
shutter	затвор	*zuttvor*
sieve	решето	*rishittor*
sign (vb)	подписать	*puddpeessart*
sign	дорожный знак	*durrorzhny znark*
signature	подпись	*portpeess*
silence	тишина	*tishinar*
silver	серебро	*siribror*
silver-plated	посеребрённый	*pussirribryonny*
simple	простой	*prustoy*
single (berth)	одноместный	*udnamyestny*
single (of journey)	в один конец	*vuddeen kunnyets*
single	неженатый (незамужняя)	*nyehzhinarty (nye hzumoozhnyaya)*
single	холостяк	*khullustyark*
sir	господин	*gusspuddeen*
sister	сестра	*syistrar*
sit	сидеть	*seedyayt*
size	размер	*razmyair*
ski (vb)	кататься на лыжах	*kuttartsa nah lyzhakh*
ski boots	лыжные ботинки	*lyzhny-yeh butteenki*
ski goggles	лыжные очки	*lyzhny-yeh uchkee*

ski instructor	инструктор по лыжному спорту	eenstrooktur puh lyzhnummoo
ski lessons/class	занятия по лыжному катанию	zunnyartiya puh lyzhnummoo
ski lift	(лыжный) подъёмник	(lyzhny) puddyomnik
ski pants	лыжные брюки	lyzhny-yeh bryooki
ski slope	горнолыжная трасса	gornolyzhnaya trarssa
ski stick	лыжная палка	lyzhnaya parlka
ski suit	лыжный костюм	lyzhny kustyoom
ski wax	лыжный воск	lyzhny vorsk
skimmed	полужирный	pulloozheerny
skin	кожа	korzha
skirt	юбка	yoopka
skis	лыжи	lyzhi
sleep (vb)	спать	spart
sleeping car	спальный вагон	sparlny vuggorn
sleeping pills	снотворные таблетки	snuttvorny-yeh tubblyetki
slide	слайд	slight
slip	комбинация	kumbinartsiya
slip road	подъезд	pudd-yest
slow	медленный	myedlinny
slow train	пассажирский поезд	pussazheerski por-yist
small	маленький	marlinki
small change	мелочи	myeluchi
smell	вонять	vunnyart
smoke	дым	dym
smoke	курить	kooreet
smoked	копчёный	kupchony
smoking compartment	купе для курящих	koopeh dlya kooryahshchikh
snake	змея	zmeeya
snorkel	шноркель	shnorkyil
snow (vb)	идёт снег	eedyot snyek
snow	снег	snyek
snow chains	цепь противоскольжения	tsep prutteevoskul lzhayniya
snug	уютный	ooyootny
soap	мыло	myla
soap box	мыльница	mylnitsa
soap powder	стиральный порошок	steerarlny purrushork
soccer (to play)	играть в футбол	eegrart ffootborl
soccer match	футбольный мяч	fooborlny myach
socket	розетка	ruzzyetka
socks	носки	nusskee
soft drink	прохладительный напиток	prukhluddeetyelny nuppeetuk
sole (of shoe)	подошва	puddorshva
sole (fish)	морской язык	murrskoy yuzzyk
solicitor	адвокат	udvukkart
someone	кто-то	ktor-tuh
something	что-то	shtor-tuh
sometimes	иногда	eenugdah
somewhere	где-то	gdyeh-ta
son	сын	syn
soon	скоро	skora
sore	нарыв	naryff
sore throat	боль в горле	borl vgorlye

sorry	извини(те)	*eezveenee(tyeh)*
sort	сорт	*sort*
soup	суп	*soop*
sour	кислый	*keesly*
sour cream	сметана	*smittarna*
source	источник	*eestorchnik*
south	юг	*yook*
souvenir	сувенир	*soovinneer*
spaghetti	спагетти	*spuggyeti*
spanner	вилочный ключ	*veeluchny klyooch*
spanner	гаечный ключ	*gigh-yechny klyooch*
spare	запас	*zupparss*
spare part	запчасть	*zuppcharst*
spare parts	запчасти	*zuppcharsti*
spare tyre	запасная шина	*zuppussnahya shina*
spare wheel	запасное колесо	*zuppussnoryeh kullissor*
speak	говорить	*guvvurreet*
special	особенный	*ussorbyuny*
specialist	специалист	*spetsialeest*
specialty	специальность	*spetsiarlnust*
speed limit	максимальная скорость	*makseemarlnaya skorust*
spell out	сказать по буквам	*skuzzart puh bookvum*
spicy	пикантный	*peekarntny*
splinter	заноза	*zunnorza*
spoon	ложка	*lorshka*
sport (to play)	заниматься спортом	*zunnimartsa sportom*
sport	спорт	*sport*
sports centre	спортивный зал	*spurrteevny zarl*
spot	место	*myesta*
sprain	вывихнуть	*vyvikhnoot*
spring	весна	*visnar*
square	площадь	*plorshchad*
square	квадратный	*kvuddrartny*
square metres	квадратный метр	*kvuddrartny myetr*
squash (to play)	играть в сквош	*eegrart fskvorsh*
stadium	стадион	*studdeeorn*
stage	сцена	*s-tsenna*
stain	пятно	*pyitnor*
stain remover	пятновыводитель	*pyitnovyvuddeetyel*
stairs	лестница	*lyaysnitsa*
stalls	зал	*zarl*
stamp	марка	*marka*
starch	крахмал	*krukhmarl*
start	завести	*zuvvistee*
station	вокзал	*vukkzarl*
statue	памятник	*parmyutnik*
stay	остановиться	*ustunnuveetsa*
stay	остаться	*ustartsa*
stay	пребывание	*prebyvarniyeh*
steal	украсть	*ookrarst*
steel	сталь	*starl*
stench	вонь	*vorn*
sting	жалить	*zharleet*
stitch (medical)	шов	*shorf*
stitch (vb)	сшить	*s-sheet*
stockings	чулки	*choolkee*
stomach	желудок	*zhilooduk*

Word list

15

stomach ache (he has)	у него болит живот	*oo nivvor bulleet zhivort*
stomach ache	боль в желудке	*borl vzhilootkyeh*
stomach cramps	колики	*korleeki*
stools	испражнение	*eespruzhnyayniyeh*
stop (vb)	остановить	*ustunnuvveet*
stop	остановка	*ustunnorfka*
stopover	промежуточная посадка	*prummizhootuch naya pussartka*
storey	этаж	*etarzh*
storm (vb)	бушевать	*booshivart*
storm	буря	*boorya*
straight	прямой	*pryummoy*
straight ahead	прямо	*pryarmo*
straw	соломинка	*sullorminka*
strawberries	клубника	*kloobneeka*
street	улица	*oolitsa*
strike (n)	забастовка	*zubbustorfka*
strong	крепкий	*kryepki*
study (vb)	учиться	*oocheetsa*
stuffing	начинка	*nucheenka*
subscriber's number	номер телефона	*normer tyeliforna*
subtitled	с субтитрами	*s-soopteetrummi*
succeed	удаться	*oodartsa*
sugar	сахар	*sarkhar*
suit	костюм	*kustyoom*
suitcase	чемодан	*chimmuddarn*
summer	лето	*lyeta*
summertime	летнее время	*lyetnyeyeh vraymya*
sun	солнце	*sorntsa*
sun hat	шляпа от солнца	*shlyappa ut sorntsa*
sunbathe	загорать	*zuggurrart*
Sunday	воскресенье	*vusskrissyaynyeh*
sunglasses	тёмные очки	*tyomny-yeh uchkee*
sunrise	восход солнца	*vusskhort sorntsa*
sunset	заход солнца	*zakkhort sorntsa*
sunstroke	солнечный удар	*sorlnyechny oodar*
suntan lotion	крем для загара	*kryem dlya zuggara*
suntan oil	масло от солнечных ожогов	*marssla ut sorlnyechnykh uzhorguff*
supermarket	универсам	*ooneevyairsarm*
surcharge	доплата	*dupplarta*
surf (vb)	заниматься серфингом	*zunneemartsa syairfingum*
surf board	доска для серфинга	*duskar dlya syairfinga*
surgery	приёмные часы	*preeyomny-yeh chussy*
surname	фамилия	*fameeliya*
surprise	сюрприз	*syoorpreess*
swallow	проглотить	*prugglutteet*
swamp	болото	*bullorta*
sweat (n)	пот	*port*
sweet	конфетка	*kunfyetka*
sweet (adj)	сладкий	*slartki*
sweetcorn	кукуруза	*kookoorooza*
sweeteners	таблетки сахарина	*tubblyetki sukhareena*
sweets	конфеты	*kunfyetty*
swim	плавать	*plarvat*
swimming bath attendant	инструктор	*eenstrooktur*
swimming pool	бассейн	*bussyayn*

Word list

15

swimming trunks	плавки	*plarfki*
swindle (n)	жульничество	*zhoolnichestsva*
switch	выключатель	*vyklyoochartyel*
synagogue	синагога	*seenuggorga*

T

table	стол	*storl*
table tennis (to play)	играть в настольный теннис	*eegrart vnustorlny tennees*
tablet	таблетка	*tubblyetka*
take (of time)	длиться	*dleetsa*
take (photograph)	фотографировать	*futtagruffeeruvvat*
take	принять	*preenyart*
taken	занятый	*zarnyaty*
talcum powder	тальк	*tarlk*
talk	говорить	*guvurreet*
tampons	тампон	*tumporn*
tanned	загорелый	*zagurryelly*
tap	кран	*krarn*
tap water	водопроводная вода	*vuddupruvvordnaya vuddar*
taste (vb)	попробовать	*pupprorbuvvart*
tax free shop	магазин беспошлинной торговли	*mugguzzeen bye sporshleenoy turrgorvli*
taxi	такси	*tukksee*
taxi stand	стоянка такси	*stuyahnka tukksee*
tea	чай	*chigh*
teapot	чайник	*chighnik*
teaspoon	чайная ложка	*chighnaya lorshka*
teat (on bottle)	соска	*sorska*
telegram	телеграмма	*tyeligrarma*
telephoto lens	телеобъектив	*tyeli-ubb-yekteef*
television set	телевизор	*tyeliveezur*
telex	телекс	*tyeleks*
temperature	температура	*tyemperutoora*
temporary filling	временная пломба	*vrayminnaya plormba*
tender (meat)	мягкий	*myakhki*
tennis (to play)	играть в теннис	*eegrart ftenniss*
tennis ball	теннисный мяч	*tennissny myach*
tennis court	теннисная площадка	*tennissnaya plushchartka*
tennis racket	теннисная ракетка	*tennissnaya rukkaytka*
tenpin bowling	играть в кегли	*eegrart fkyegli*
tent	палатка	*pullartka*
tent peg	колышек	*korlyshek*
terrace	терраса	*tyairarssa*
terrible	ужасно	*oozharssna*
terribly	чрезвычайно	*chryayzvychighno*
thank	благодарить	*bluggadurreet*
thank you	спасибо	*spasseeba*
thanks	спасибо	*spasseebo*
thaw (vb)	таять	*tahyart*
theatre	театр	*tee-artr*
theft	кража	*krarzha*
there	там	*tarm*
thermal bath	термическая ванна	*tyairmeecheskaya varna*
thermometer	термометр	*tyairmormyetr*
thick	толстый	*torlsty*
thief	вор	*vorr*

Word list

15

thigh	бедро	*byidror*
thin	тонкий	*tornki*
thin	худой	*khoodoy*
things	вещи	*vyayshchi*
think	думать	*doomat*
third (n)	треть	*tryet*
thirst	жажда	*zharzhda*
this afternoon	сегодня днём	*sivvordnya dnyom*
this evening	сегодня вечером	*sivvordnya vyaychirum*
this morning	сегодня утром	*sivvordnya ootrum*
thread	нитка (ниточка)	*neetka (neetuchka)*
thread	нить	*neet*
throat	горло	*gorla*
throat lozenges	таблетки для горла	*tubblyetki dlya gbla*
throwing up	меня рвёт	*minya rvyort*
thunderstorm	гроза	*gruzzar*
Thursday	четверг	*chitvyairk*
ticket (admission)	билет	*beelyet*
ticket (travel)	билет	*beelyet*
tickets	билеты	*beelyety*
tidy	убрать	*oobrart*
tie	галстук	*garlsstuk*
tights	колготки	*kulgortki*
time	время	*vraymya*
times	раз	*rarss*
timetable	расписание	*rasspeessarniye*
tin	банка	*barnka*
tip	на чай	*nah chigh*
toast	тост	*torst*
tobacco	табак	*tubbark*
tobacconist's shop	табачная лавка	*tubbarchnaya larfka*
toboggan (n)	сани	*sarni*
today	сегодня	*sivvordnya*
toe	палец	*parlyets*
together	вместе	*vmyestyeh*
toilet	туалет	*too-ullyet*
toilet paper	туалетная бумага	*too-uhlyetnaya boomarga*
toiletries	туалетные принадлежности	*too-uhlyetny-yeh preenuddlyezhnusti*
tomato	помидор	*pummeedor*
tomato purée	томатное пюре	*tummartnoyeh pyooray*
tomato sauce	(томатный) кетчуп	*(tummartny) kyetchoop*
tomorrow	завтра	*zarftra*
tongue	язык	*yuzzyk*
tonic water	тоник	*tornik*
tonight	сегодня ночью	*sivvordnya norchyoo*
too much	слишком много	*sleeshkum mnorga*
tools	инструменты	*eenstroomyenty*
tooth	зуб	*zoop*
toothache	зубная боль	*zoobnahya borl*
toothbrush	зубная щётка	*zoobnahya shchotka*
toothpaste	зубная паста	*zoobnahya parsta*
toothpick	зубочистка	*zoobocheestka*
top up	дополнить	*dupporlneet*
total	общий	*orbshchi*
tough	жёсткий	*zhostki*
tour	прогулка	*pruggoolka*

Word list

15

English	Russian	Pronunciation
tour guide	гид	*geet*
tourist card	туристическая карта	*tooreesteecheskaya karta*
tourist class	туристский класс	*tooreestski klarss*
Tourist Information Office	туристическое бюро	*tooreesteecheskoyeh byooror*
tourist menu	меню для туристов	*minyoo dlya tooreestuff*
tow (vb)	взять на буксир	*vzyart nah bookseer*
tow cable	буксир	*bookseer*
towel	полотенце	*pullutyentseh*
tower	башня	*barshnya*
town hall	ратуша	*rartoosha*
town city	город	*gorut*
toy	игрушка	*eegrooshka*
traffic	движение	*dveezhaybniyeh*
traffic light	светофор	*svyetafor*
train	поезд	*por-yist*
train ticket	билет (на поезд)	*beelyet (nah por-yist)*
train timetable	расписание поездов	*russpeessarniyeh puh-yizdorff*
training shoes	кроссовки	*krussorfki*
translate	перевести	*pirivisstee*
travel (vb)	путешествовать	*pootyeshestvvuvvart*
travel agent	бюро путешествий	*byooror pootyeshestviy*
travel guide	путеводитель	*pootyevuddeetyel*
traveller	путешественник	*pootyeshestvennik*
traveller's cheque	дорожный чек	*durrorzhny chyek*
treacle/syrup	патока	*partukka*
treatment	лечение	*lichayniye*
tree	дерево	*dyayrivva*
triangle	треугольник	*tray-oogorlnik*
trim	подстричь	*puddstreech*
trip	экскурсия	*ekskoorseeya*
trip	путешествие	*pootyeshestviyeh*
trip	поездка	*puhyestka*
troubled by	его беспокоит	*yivor byespukkor-eet*
trousers	брюки	*bryooki*
trout	форель	*furrel*
trunk call	междугородный	*myezhdoogurrordny*
trunk code	код (города)	*kort (gorudda)*
trustworthy	надёжный	*nuddyozhny*
try on	примерить	*preemyaireet*
tube	тюбик	*tyoobik*
Tuesday	вторник	*ftornik*
tumble drier	сушилка	*soosheelka*
tuna	тунец	*toonyets*
tunnel	туннель	*toonel*
turn	раз	*rahss*
TV	телевизор	*tyeliveezur*
TV and radio guide	программа радио- и телепередач	*pruggrarma rahdeeo- ee*
tweezers	пинцет	*peentset*
tyre	покрышка (шины)	*pukkryshka (shiny)*
tyre lever	монтажная лопатка для шин	*muntarzhnaya lup-partka dlya shin*

Word list

15

U

umbrella	зонтик	*zorntik*
under	под	*pudd*
underground	метро	*myitror*
underground railway system	сеть метрополитена	*syayt myitruppullitayna*
underground station	станция метро	*starntsiya mitror*
underpants	трусы	*troossy*
understand	понять	*punnyart*
underwear	нижнее бельё	*neezhnyeyeh billyor*
undress	раздеть	*ruzzdyayt*
unemployed	безработный	*byezrubbortny*
uneven	неровный	*nyehrorvny*
university	университет	*ooneevairsityayt*
unleaded	без свинца	*byes sveentsah*
up	наверх	*nuvvyairkh*
urgency	поспешность	*pusspyeshnust*
urgent	срочный	*srorchny*
urine	моча	*muchar*
use	использовать	*eessporlzuvvart*
usually	чаще всего	*charshcher vsivvor*

V

vacate	освободить	*ussvubbudeet*
vaccinate	привить	*preeveet*
vagina	влагалище	*vluggarleeshcheh*
vaginal infection	влагалищная инфекция	*vluggarleeshch naya eenfyektseeya*
valid	действующий	*dyaystvooyushchi*
valley	долина	*dulleena*
valuable	дорогой	*durrugoy*
van	фургон	*foorgorn*
vanilla	ваниль	*vunneel*
vase	ваза	*varza*
vaseline	вазелин	*vazilleen*
veal	телятина	*tilyartina*
vegetable soup	овощной суп	*uvvushchnoy soop*
vegetables	овощи	*orvushchi*
vegetarian	вегетарианец	*vegeturreeahnyets*
vehicle documents	технический паспорт	*tyekhneecheski parsspurt*
vein	вена	*vyenna*
venereal disease	венерическая болезнь	*vyenereecheskaya bullyezn*
vermin	вредители	*vrideetyeli*
via	через	*chayruss*
video recorder	видеомагнитофон	*videeomuggneetufforn*
video tape	видеоплёнка	*videeoplyonka*
view	вид	*veet*
village	деревня	*dirayvnya*
visa	виза	*veeza*
visit	посетить	*pussiteet*
visit	гости	*gorsti*
vitamin tablets	таблетки витамина	*tubblyetki veetummeena*
vitamins	витамины	*veetummeeny*
vodka	водка	*vortka*
volcano	вулкан	*voolkarn*
volleyball	играть в волейбол	*eegrart v vullayborl*
vomit	рвать	*r-vart*

W

wait	ждать	*zhdart*
waiter	официант	*uffitsiarnt*
waiting room	зал ожидания	*zarl uzhidarniya*
waitress	официантка	*uffitsiarntka*
wake up	разбудить	*ruzzboodeet*
Wales	Уэльс	*Oo-ellss*
walk (n)	прогулка	*prugoolka*
walk	гулять	*goolyart*
wallet	бумажник	*boomarzhnik*
wardrobe	гардероб	*gardyirorp*
warm	тёплый	*tyoply*
warn	предупредить	*pridooprideet*
warning	предупреждение	*pridooprizhdyayn iyeh*
wash (clothes)	стирать	*steerart*
washing-powder	моющее средство	*mor-yooshchiyeh sryetstva*
washing	бельё	*bilyor*
washing line	бельевая верёвка	*bilyevahya viryofka*
washing machine	стиральная машина	*steerarlnaya mushina*
wasp	оса	*ussar*
water	вода	*vuddar*
water melon	арбуз	*arbooss*
water ski (vb)	кататься на водных лыжах	*kuttartsa nah vordnykh lyzhakh*
waterproof	водонепроницаемый	*vuddanyehprunnitsahye my*
wave-pool	бассейн с искусственными волнами	*bussayn skoostvinnymi*
way	средство	*sraytstva*
we	мы	*my*
weak	слабый	*slarby*
weather	погода	*puggorda*
weather forecast	прогноз погоды	*prugnorss puggordy*
wedding	свадьба	*svardba*
Wednesday	среда	*sriddar*
week	неделя	*nidyaylya*
weekend	выходные (дни)	*vykhuddnyyeh (dnee)*
weekend duty	в эти выходные он работает	*vehti vykhudnyyeh orn rubortayeht*
weekly ticket	абонемент на неделю	*abbunnimyent nah nidyaylyu*
welcome	добро пожаловать	*dubbror puzharluvvat*
well (advb)	хорошо	*khurushor*
Welsh (adj)	валлийский	*vulleesski*
Welshman	валлиец	*vulleeyets*
Welshwoman	валлийка	*vulleeka*
west	запад	*zarput*
wet	мокрый	*morkry*
wetsuit	костюм для серфинга	*kustyoom dlya syairfinga*
what is the problem?	на что вы жалуетесь?	*na shtor vy zharlooyetyes?*
what?	что?	*shtor?*
wheel	колесо	*kullissor*
wheelchair	инвалидное кресло	*eenvulleednuhyeh kraysla*
when?	когда?	*kugdar?*
where?	где?	*gdyeh?*
which?	какой?	*kukkoy?*
whipped cream	взбитые сливки	*vzbeety-yeh sleefki*

Word list

white	белый	*byely*
who?	кто?	*ktor?*
wholemeal	из муки грубого помола	*eess mookee groobuvva pummorla*
wholemeal bread	хлеб грубого помола	*khlyep groobuvva pummorla*
why?	почему?	*puchimoo?*
wide-angle lens	широкоугольный объектив	*shirorka-oogorlny ubbyekteef*
widow	вдова	*vduvvar*
widower	вдовец	*vduvvyets*
wife	жена	*zhinnar*
wild strawberries	земляника	*zimlyuneeka*
wind	ветер	*vyaytyer*
windbreak	ветровой щит	*vitruvvoy shcheet*
windmill	мельница	*myelneetsa*
window	окно	*uknor*
windscreen wiper	дворник	*dvornik*
wine	вино	*veenor*
wine list	меню алкогольных напитков	*minyoo ullkuggorl nykh nuppeetkuff*
winter	зима	*zeemar*
witness	свидетель	*svidyaytyel*
woman	женщина	*zhenshchinna*
wool	шерсть	*shairst*
word	слово	*slorva*
work	работа	*rubborta*
working day	рабочий день	*rubborchiy dyen*
worn	поношенный	*punnorshunny*
worried (to be)	волноваться	*vullnuvvartsa*
wound	рана	*rarna*
wrap	завернуть	*zuvvirnoot*
write	писать	*peessart*
write down	записать	*zuppeessart*
writing pad	блокнот	*blukknort*
writing paper	почтовая бумага	*puchtorvaya boomarga*
written	письменный	*peesmunny*
wrong	неправильный	*nyeh-prarveelny*

Y

yacht	яхта	*yarkhta*
year	год	*gort*
yellow	жёлтый	*zholty*
yes	да	*dah*
yes please	с удовольствием	*sooduvvorlstviyem*
yesterday	вчера	*vchirar*
yoghurt	кефир	*kyeffeer*
you	вы	*vy*
you too	вам того же	*varm tuvvor zheh*
youth hostel	молодёжная турбаза	*mulludyozhnaya turbarza*

Z

zip	молния	*morlneeya*
zoo	зоопарк	*zuh-uhpark*

Word list

15

Basic grammar

There are no *the* and *a/an* words in Russian. Thus **дом** (dorm) can mean 'the house', 'a house', or plain 'house'. Prefixing the noun with **этот/тот** (etut - tort - this/that) is often useful: **этот/тот дом** (etut/tort dorm - this/that house).

Russian has three genders: masculine, feminine and neuter. As a rule, nouns that end in a consonant are masculine, e.g. **чемодан** (chimma**darn** - a suitcase); nouns ending in **-а** or **-yah** are feminine, e.g. **девушка** (d**yay**vooshka - a girl) and **тётя** (t**yo**tya - aunt); nouns ending in **-o** or **-yeh** are neuter, e.g. **окно** (ukkn**or** - window) and **море** (m**or**yeh - sea).

Adjectives must agree in gender with the nouns they go with:

masculine adjectival ending **-ый** (**-y**) or **-ой** (**-oy**), therefore **красивый дом** (kruss**ee**vy dorm - beautiful house), **молодой человек** (mullodd**oy** chillov**ye**k - young man);

feminine adjectival ending **-ая** (**-aya**), therefore **красивая девушка** (kruss**ee**vaya dy**ay**vooshka - beautiful girl);

neuter adjectival ending **-oe** (**-or-yeh**), therefore **красивое море** (kruss**ee**vor-yeh m**or**yeh - beautiful sea).

In the plural there is a single form **-ые** (**y-yeh**) for all genders:

красивые дома	(kruss**ee**vy-yeh dumm**ar** - beautiful houses)
красивые девушки	(kruss**ee**vy-yeh dy**ay**vooshki - beautiful girls)
красивые моря	(kruss**ee**vy-yeh murr**ya** - beautiful seas)

Much of the complexity of Russian derives from the fact that nouns, pronouns and adjectives also change according to which of six 'cases' (nominative, accusative, genitive etc.) they are in, and according to gender and number— far too intricate for a basic grammar!

In this phrasebook it is generally the masculine form that is given, but wherever necessary the feminine form is also given in brackets. This is especially necessary when you are using the past tense, which is basically a form of the verb ending in 'l':

я был	*ya byl*	I (a man) was
я прочитал	*ya pruchitarl*	I (a man) have read
я была	*ya bylah*	I (a woman) was
я прочитала	*ya pruchitarla*	I (a woman) have read
это было	*ettuh bylo*	it (a thing) was
море было	*moryeh bylo*	the sea (neuter noun) was.

In other words, in the past the verb ends in '**l**' for masculine singular, '**-la**' for feminine singular, and '**-lo**' for neuter singular. For the plural there is one ending, '**-lee**':

мы были	*my bylee*	we were

In the present, Russian does not use a verb 'to be'. Thus **он врач** (*orn vrarch* - he doctor) means 'he is a doctor', and **она красивая девушка** (*unnah krusseevaya dyayvooshka* - she beautiful girl) means 'she is a beautiful girl'. To say 'I am' etc, you need just the pronouns:

я	*ya*	I (am)
ты	*ty*	you (informal form) (are)
он/она/оно	*orn/unnah/unnor*	he/she/it (is)
мы	*my*	we (are)
вы	*vy*	you (formal/plural) (are)
они	*unnee*	they (are)

The verb 'to have' is rendered by a prepositional construction meaning roughly 'there is about me':

у меня есть	*oo minyah yest*	I have
у тебя есть	*oo tibbyah yest*	you (informal form) have
у него есть	*oo nyivvor yest*	he has
у неё есть	*oo nyeeyor yest*	she has
у него есть	*oo nyivvor yest*	it has
у нас есть	*oo narss yest*	we have
у вас есть	*oo varss yest*	you (formal/plural) have
у них есть	*oo neekh yest*	they (masc/fem/neut) have